A Garland Series

The English Stage
Attack and Defense 1577 - 1730

A collection of 90 important works
reprinted in photo-facsimile in 50 volumes

edited by
Arthur Freeman
Boston University

The Second Part of
the Anatomie of Abuses

by

Phillip Stubbes

with a preface
for the Garland Edition by

Arthur Freeman

Garland Publishing, Inc., New York & London

1973

Copyright © 1973

by Garland Publishing, Inc.

All Rights Reserved

Library of Congress Cataloging in Publication Data

Stubbes, Phillip.
    The second part of the anatomie of abuses.

    (The English stage: attack and defense 1577-1730)
    Reprint of the 1583 ed. printed by R. W. for W.
Wright, London.
    1. Theater--Moral and religious aspects. 2. Theater
--England. I. Title. II. Series.
PN2047.S82 1973   792'.013   73-4399
ISBN 0-8240-0591-0

Preface

The "second part" of Phillip Stubbes's Anatomie *is really an independent work, unpredicted in the original compilation of "abuses," but nonetheless of obvious relevance to the better-known antitheatrical tract. It was registered six months after "part one" on 7 November 1583, and appeared in that year; but unlike "part one"— perhaps because its publisher was not Richard Jones—it was never incorporated in a "complete" edition, nor republished singly. E. K. Chambers,* Elizabethan Stage, *IV, 221, says that "part two" "has not been reprinted," but in fact it was, with an eccentric apparatus and introduction, by F. J. Furnivall for the* New Shakespere Society, *1882.*

We reprint British Museum 697.a.35 (2), collating A⁸ [lacks A1 blank]B-P⁸, a catchword on G3 cropped. There is a variant issue, with cancel title and all the preliminaries cancelled, exemplified by British Museum Grenville 10370; we reprint the title as an appendix. Furnivall unfortunately chose to edit this truncated version, and so his text is

incomplete. Altogether six copies (British Museum, Lambeth, Oxford [2]; Folger, Newberry) are recorded of the first issue.
   STC *23380; not in Lowe-Arnott-Robinson.*

January, 1973   A.F.

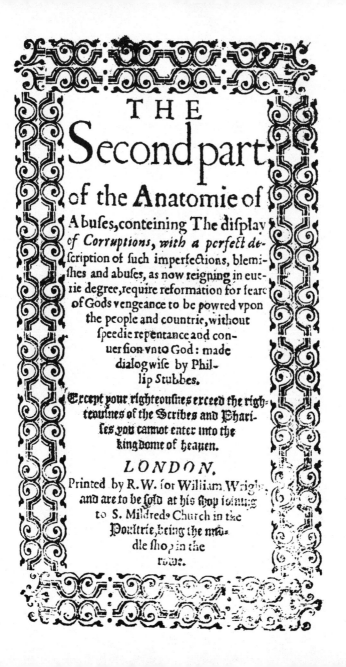

THE
Second part,
of the **Anatomie** of

Abuses, conteining The display
of *Corruptions*, with a perfett de-
scription of such imperfections, blemishes and abuses, as now reigning in euerie degree, require reformation for feare
of Gods vengeance to be powred vpon
the people and countrie, without
speedie repentance and con-
uersion vnto God: made
dialogwise by Phil-
lip Stubbes.

Except your righteousnes exceed the righteousnes of the Scribes and Phari-
ses, you cannot enter into the
kingdome of heauen.

LONDON.

Printed by R. W. for William Wright,
and are to be sold at his shop ioining
to S. Mildreds Church in the
Poultrie, being the mid-
dle shop in the
rowe.

To the chriſtian Reader, grace, mercie and peace.

Here was neuer any age, or time (chriſtian reader) ſince the beginning of the world how corrupt ſo euer, that was comparable to this our thriſe vnhappie age in all kind of corruption, wickednes, and ſin, with greefe of conſcience I ſpeake it, with weeping eies I behold it, and with ſorrowfull hart I lament it. And therefore ſeeing wickedneſſe doth ſo abound, the Lord (leaſt his children froſen in the dregs of their ſinne ſhould periſh with the wicked) raiſeth vp in his mercie good men (as we ſee he hath done our good brother the author hereof) to plucke off the viſors of ſinne from their faces, and to lay them open to the view of the whole world, to the end that euerie one ſeeing the dung of his wicked waies, and the filthie dregs of ſinne throwne in their faces, may bluſh at the ſame, be aſhamed, repent, amend, and turne to the Lord Ieſus, and ſo eternally be ſaued To this end and purpoſe hath the author hereof (for whoſe ſingular towardnes in his primar yeres the Lord Ieſus be praiſed) taken in hand the compiling of this little treatiſe, conteining a ſummarie of certeine corruptions and abuſes, as well in the temporaltie, as in the clergie. Wherefore good Reader read ouer the ſame mature, aduiſedly, iudge of the

ſame

same imparcially, and at no hand condemne not re-
mere, rashly, but compare euery thing with the truth
of Gods word, and the state of time, and as it shall
agree or disagree from the word of God, so to like or
dislike of the same. For I am persuaded that there is
nothing comprised in this whole booke, but what is
agreeable to the word of God, sauing that in a few
points the author bearing with the infirmitie of the
time, hath somwhat qualified both his stile and matter, in hope of speedie reformation to insue, which
God grant. Therefore gentle Reader, let me obtaine
thus much at thy hands, as to accept his good meaning, as well towards the truth, as towards the professors thereof, to rest thankfull to God for him, and
to helpe him with thy praiers, that as hitherto euen
from his youth he hath borne a zeale to the truth
of Christs religion, so he may continue to the
end, expressing (as he hath begun) in life
and conuersation for euer through
Christ Iesus our onlie Lord
and Sauiour. A-
men.

Thy fellowe laborer. I. F.

¶ To the Right
HONORABLE,
and his singular good Lord
Phillip Earle of Arundell,
Phillip Stubs wisheth all prosperitie
in this life, with increase of ho-
nour, and eternall felicitie in
the heauenlie hierar-
chie by Iesus
Christ.

Auing made the first part of
the Anatomie of abuses (Right honorable, and my verie good Lord)
and dedicated the same to your good
Lordship, I thought I should then
haue taken mine Vltimum vale, for
euer-needing to write anie more of
this argument againe. But seeing the diuell our ancient aduersarie in the fulnesse of his malice hath since
spued out his poison. and powred out his filthie dregs
of infinit corruptions, blemishes, and abuses (al which

to comprehend in number were Infinitum finito comprehendere) amongst vs of late daies more than euer were heard of before. I was compelled for the health of their soules, and benefit of my countrey. to take in hand afresh this new tractation, intituled The display of Corruptions, wherein are laid open diuers and sundrie abuses, corruptions, and blemishes crept as well into one sort of men as into another. And hauing finished the same, and committed it to the presse, I stood in suspense, douting to whom I might dedicate the same, as well for the argument, and matter which it handeleth (being a botch, which some frosen in the dregges of their sinne cannot in any wise abide to be touched) as also for the inhability and indignitie of the author But at the last considering with my selfe the proximitie, the semblance, and neerenesse of the arguments, as well of my first booke of the Anatomie of abuses, as also of this the Display of Corruptions, I could doe no lesse than to dedicate the same to your excellent Lordship, to the end, that your Honour (whom the Lord hath made the mirrour of true nobilitie) might see, as it were in a glasse) a briefe summarie of the corruptions and abuses that reigne in these daies. And not onely for this cause was I incited to commit the defense of this little treatise to your Honourable Lordship, but also and in especiall, in demonstration of my thankfull hart, and vnfained goodwill towardes your Honour. in that it pleased the same (farre beyond either my desart or expectation) not onely to accept, and take in good part my former simple booke of the Anatomie of Abuses, but also most honourably to shield the same vnder the wings and guardance of your Lordships protection. In recompense whereof, if mine habilitie were answerable to my
faithful

faithfull hart, and goodwill borne to your Honor, then should this present gift be as great, as now by reason of the contrarie it is small and contemptible. And although I may be adiudged of som to be ouer presumptuous in dedicating this booke vnto your Honour, yet if they will consider, that such treatises as this (and especially in these corrupt daies, wherein no man can abide to heare of his faults) are not to be dedicated to euery one without exception, but to such whom GOD hath blessed (as his glorious name be praised therefore he hath done your Honour) with all graces and gifts either spirituall, or corporall whatsoeuer. And therfore haue I had a special regard, that as this my booke doth discouer and lay open to the view of the world, manie and sundrie corruptions, abuses, and blemishes in euery degree, so I might dedicate the same to one free from all the same blemishes and corruptions, least otherwise it might happily be a pricke to his eies, and an offense to his mind. For this (right Honourable and my very good Lord) I hold for a Maxime, that he who is licenciously and dissolutely inclined, can hardly in any sauce brooke or digest good bookes, which reproue such things as he so greedily thirsteth after. This maketh many a one of a giltie conscience (when he cannot abide to heare his faults ript vp, bicause he is faultie) to cast away good bookes, and to contemne both them and the authors, who with great studie labour and paines haue finished the same for the glorie of GOD, and benefit of their country. But had euery one tasted of the fauourable acceptation of their patrones, to whose tuition they commend their labours, as wel as I haue of your good Lordships, not onely acceptation, but also most bountifull remuneration, they should not neede to feare any

refusall

refusall of their faithfull good wils in exhibiting good
works vnto their protection and defense. Which thing
though I can neuer sufficiently in effect regraciate, yet
in effect I will not faile (Christ willing)to the end of
my life faithfully to supply. And truly not without
great cause am I bound so to doe, and not onely I, but
euen all that in any respect haue to deale with your honorable Lordship. For what is the common bruit nwised
of your Honour? Truly this. That your Lordship for
gentlenesse and affabilitie (whereof I haue tasted to
my singular comfort)is surpassing any, in good conscience, mercie, and compassion inferiour to none, in noble
prowesse, valiancie, & magnanimitie comparable with
the best. In wisedome and vnderstanding singular, in
zeale to the truth and christian religion famous, in defending of equitie and iustice renowmed. Finally, in all
kind of vertue equall with any, so as I will not feare
to call your good Lordship a perfect patterne of true
nobilitie in all respects. Thus hauing rather as the
peinter doth, to draw the lineaments of your Lordships
vertues with my rude pensill, than to display the liuely
proport on of the whole bodie thereof,which is vnpossible, I will surcease the same For if I should take vpon me to discipher foorth the whole bodie of your Lordships deserued commendations, I should rather not
knowe where to end,than where to begin. But least I
might seeme to aggrauate your sacred eares, occupied
with grauer and sager matters than these,I will draw
to an end, most humbly beseeching your good Lordship
to receiue this little treatise into your Honors patronage, with like plausible alacritie, as your Honour receiued my former dedication. And not only to receiue the
same into your Lordships protection, but also to remaine

maine the iuſt defender thereof againſt the filthie crew
of ſlowting Momus , and railing Zoilus, with their
complices of bragging Thraſos, and wrangling Phormions, to whom as the Greeke prouerbe ſaith: μωμι-
σέϳαι τις θασσον εμιμεσέϳαι, It is eaſier to carp,
& to find fault with, than to imitate, or amend. And thus
crauing pardon at your good Lordſhips hand, for this
my bold attempt, I moſt humbly take my leaue, committing your Honor with my good Ladie your wife,
and all the reſt of your honorable progenie, and aliance
to the tuition and protection of the bleſſed God, who
keepe and preſerue the ſame, in his faith, feare,
and loue all the daies of your life, with in-
creaſe of much honour, and eter-
nall beatitude in the heauens by Ieſus
Chriſt.

Your Honors moſt humble, and

Obedient to command,

Phillip Stubbes.

The Author to the
gentle Reader.

Am conſtrained (gentle rea-
der) before I go any further
to make this requeſt vnto
thee. That whereſoeuer
thou ſhalt chance in the
reading of this little trea-
tiſe, to finde any faults or eſcapes either in
the print, or in the matter (as there be too
many) thou wilt either friendly beare with
them, or elſe curteouſly amend them with
thy penne. And if it be ſo, that any poſi-
tion or aſſumption in any part of my boke
doe ſeeme ſtrange vnto thee (as manye
things may doe peraduenture at the firſt
bluſh , eſpecially being vttered in theſe
dainty daies) that thou wilt of thy friendly curteſie, and zeale which thou beareſt
to the truth, to the glorie of God, to good
letters, and to the edification of the church
of G O D, either expunge them with thy
penne, qualifie them with the oile of thy
fauorable

fauorable iudgement, or elſe at the leaſt ſo
to conſtrue & interpret them as they both
may ſtand with the truth, with the time,
and with the minde, good meaning, and
intent of the author, whoſe minde was (I
call heauen and earth to witneſſe) to profit all, and to offend none . And therefore
if any bee offended at any thing in this
booke, it is *Scandalum acceptum, non da-
tum,* Offenſe taken, not giuen. For the
auoiding whereof (God is my iudge, who
knoweth the ſecrets of all harts) I haue
abſtained from ſome things which I ought
to haue ſpoken of, and otherſome which
I haue ſpoken of, I haue ſo qualified, that
I may ſeeme rather to beare with the corruption of the time, than the truth of the
cauſe, aud rather to loue any thing better
than ſchiſmes & diſſentions in the church
of GOD, about matters of ſmall importance. Therefore (good Reader) in chriſtian charitie I beſeech thee to reſpect my
ſimple meaning, which was to ſet foorth
the glorie of Chriſt Ieſus, and the truth of
his word, to the edifieng of his militant
church vpon the earth, and withall to conſider the marke that I ſhoot at (namelie,

to

to infinuate the truth, and to weede out all corruptions, &c.) the end, and purpofe of my drift, and to defend this little booke againft flouting *Momus*, bragging *Thrafos*, and wrangling *Phormions*, *Quibus omnia bona odio habentur*, to whom al good things are had in contempt. Thus I commit thee to God (moft Chriftian reader) and to the power of his might, who bleffe thee with all graces fpirituall and corporall in this life, that long maift thou read, and much maift thou profit, and in the end grant thee eternall life in the heauens, thy inheritance purchafed with the bodie of Chrift Iefus, to whom be praife, glorie, honour, and dominion in all congregations for euer.
Amen.

Thine to his power in the Lord to command,

Phillip Stubbes.

I.S, in commendation of the Author, *and his booke.*

THe ſtate of theſe vnhappie daies,
    alas lament we may :
Sith that the ſame ſo fraughted are,
    with wickednes ech way.

O England deere, my natiue ſoile,
    I ſorie am for thee :
For that thou wilt not leaue thy ſinne,
    and eke repentant bee.

But day by day, from naught to worſe,
    thou daily doſt proceed:
Both temporaltie and clergie they,
    to worke ſinne haue decreed.

Haſt thou forgot there is a God,
    that wickedneſſe doth hate :
And who will one day puniſh it,
    in ech degree and ſtate ?

And doſt thou not remember well,
    the dangers manifold :
Wherein of late thou ſtoodeſt (alas)
    more than can well be told ?

And haſt thou alſo cleane forgot,
    and out of mind let fall :
How that the goodnes ot thy God,
    deliuerd thee from all.

                       Praiſe

Praise him therefore with hart and voice,
   shew not thy selfe vnkinde,
And let not these his mercies great,
   fall out of gratefull minde.

His iudgements great are towards thee,
   his mercies are much more :
And all to allure thee from thy sinne,
   his name be praisd therefore.

Let either thone, or thother then ,
   mooue thee to leaue thy sinne :
Then God to powre his blessings store,
   vpon thee shall not linne.

Read ouer then this little booke,
   and that with single eie :
And thou the state of this our age,
   as in a glasse shalt see.

Be warnd therefore, thy life amend,
   while thou hast time and space :
That in the end in heauen blisse,
   thou maist haue thy solace.

Thine in the Lord, I. S.

THE DISPLAY OF
corruptions, requiring reformation *for feare of Gods iudge-*
ments to be powred vpon the people
and country without spee-
die amendement.

The speakers THEODORVS and
AMPHILOGVS.

GOD blesse you my
friend, and well ouer-
taken.

Amphilogus. You are
hartilie welcome good
sir with all my hart.

Theod. How farre
purpose you to trauell
this way by the grace

of God?

Amphil. As far as Nodnol if God permit.

Theod. What place is that I pray you,
and where is it scituate?

Amphil. It is a famous citie, and the chiefest place in Dnalgne, haue you not heard of it?

Theod. No truely. For I am a stranger,
and newly come into these conntries, onely to
sie fashions, and to learne the state and condi-

tion

tion of those things whereof I am ignozant.

Amphil. What country man are you, I pzay you, if I may be so bold as to aske?

Theod. I am of the country and nation of the Idumeans, a cruell, fierce, and seruile kind of people.

Amphil. I haue bæne in those countries my selfe ere now, and therefoze it is maruell that you knowe me not.

Theod. Me thinke I should knowe you, but yet I cannot call your name to remembzance.

Amphil. My name is Amphilogus somtime of your acquaintance, though now you haue (thzough tract of time, which is Omniũ rerum edax, I deuourer of al things) fozgot the same. But notwithstanding that you haue fozgot me, yet I remember you very well : is not your name Maister Theodorus?

Theod. Pes truly my name is Theodorus, I neither can, noz yet will euer deniz the same.

Amphil. What make you in these countries, if I may aske you without offence?

Theod. Truly I came hither to sæ the country, people, and nation, to learne the tong, and to sæ (as I told you) the state generally of all things.

Amphil.

Amphil. Pou are moſt hartily welcome, and I hauing bœne a traueler, bozne in theſe countries, and knowing the ſtate thereof in euerie reſpect, to congratulate your comming, will impart vnto you the ſubſtance and effect therof in as few wozds as I can.

Theod. I pzaie you then giue me leaue (vnder cozrection) to aſke you ſuch neceſſary queſtions, as are incident to my purpoſe, and which may ſerue foz my better inſtruction in all the fozeſaide pzemiſſes?

Amphil. Go to then, aſke on in the name of God, and I will addzeſſe my ſelfe to ſatiſfie your reaſonable requeſts in any thing I can.

Theod. What be the inhabiters of this countrie? Be they a vertuous, godlie, and religious kinde of people, oz otherwiſe cleane contrarie:

Amphil. Surely they are as all other countries and nations be foz the moſt part, inclined to ſinne, and wickednes, dzinking vp iniquitie as it were water, but yet I am perſuaded that albeit all fleſh hath cozrupted his way befoze the face of G O D, yet is there not any nation oz countrey vnder the ſunne that foz pzide, whozedome, dzœnkennes, gluttonie and all kinde of oppzeſſion, iniurie, and miſchiefe, may compare with this one country of Dnalgne, God be mercifull vnto it, and haſten his kingdome that all wickednes may be done away.

Theod. Then as in all other countries, where euer I haue trauelled, ſo in this also, is verified the old adage, namely, that the firſt age of the world was called Aurea ætas, the golden age, for that men liued godlie, & in the feare of God, the second age was called Argentea ætas, the ſiluer age, for that men began ſomewhat to decline, and fall from their former holineſſe, and integritie of life, to ſinne and wickednes: the thirde and laſt age, which is this that we are fallen into, is and may iuſtlie be called Ferrea or Plumbea ætas, the yron or leaden age, in as much as now men are fallen from all godlineſſe whatſoeuer, and are as it were wedded to iniquitie, committing ſinne without any remorſe, and running into all kinde of abhomination and impietie, without reſtraint. All which things dulie in the good hart of a faithful chriſtian conſidered, & weied, may eaſilie perſuade a wiſe man to think their deſtruction to be at hand, except they repent.

Amphil. You ſaie verie well. Therfore I would wiſh them to take heed to themſelues, and to leaue their wickednes before the Lords wrath be gon out againſt them, for let them be
ſure,

sure, that when the measure of their wicked-
nesse is full, then will the Lord cut them off
from the face of the earth if they repent not,
and truely turne to the Lord. The wise man
saith, that a little before destruction come, the
hart of man shall swell into pride, and wickednes. Our sauiour Christ saith, when men flatter themselues, and saie peace, peace, al things
are well, we neede not to feare any thing, then
euen then shall sudden destruction fall vpon
them, as sorrow commeth vpon a woman tra-
uelling with childe, and they shall not escape,
bicause they would not knowe the Lord, nor
the day of his visitation. Which thing we see
to be true through al the histories of the sacred
Bible, for when the Sodomits, and Gomorreans had filled vp the measures of their iniquitie, and saciate themselues in sinne, then came
there fire and brimstone raining from heauen vpon them, and their citie, and consumed
them all, from the vpper face of the earth.
When all the worlde in the daies of Noah,
was giuen ouer to sinne, and wickednes, im-
mediatelie came the floud of Gods vengeance,
and destroied them all, eight persons to wit,
Noah, his wife, his three sonnes, and their
wiues, who serued the Lord in true simplicity
of hart, onelie excepted. The Hierosolimitanes

B.3.　　　　　when

when their sinne was ripe, were they not confounded, and put to the edge of the sworde? When Pharao the king of Egypt his sinne was ripe, did not the Lord harden his hart to pursue the Israelits, and so drowned him, and all his retinue in the read sea? Herod and Nabuchadnezer swelling in sinne, and rising vp against the maiestie of God in the malice of their harts, was not the one stroken dead in a moment, and eaten vp with worms, the other deposed from his kingdome, and constrained to eate grasse with the beasts of the earth, with the like cramples, which for the auoiding of prolixitie, I omit. By all which it appeareth, that when destruction is nærest, then are the people the securest, and the most indurate and frosen in the dregs of their sinne, and being so, the sequele is either confusion in this life, or perdition in the world to come, or both. And therefore I besæch the Lord that both this country, and all others may repent, & amende euerie one their wicked waies, to the glorie of God and their owne saluation.

Theod. Is this country fruitfull, and plenty of all things or barren, and emptie?

Amphil. There is no nation or country in the world, that for store, and abundance of all things, may compare with the same, for
                                                        of

of all things there is such plentie (God haue the praise thereof) as they may séeme to haue néede of no other nation, but al others of them. In so much as if they were wise people (as they be wise inough, if they would vse their wisedome well) to kéepe their owne substance within themselues, and not to transport it ouer to other countries (as many couetous wretches for their owne priuate gaine doe) they might liue richly and in abundance of all things, whilest other countries should languish and want. But hereof more shall be spoken hereafter.

Theod. I pray you how is this country adiacent, vpon other countries?

Amphil. It lieth inuironed with the occean sea rounde about, vpon the one side eastwarde, it bordereth vpon the confines of France : vpon the other side westward, vpon Irelande, towards the septentrionall or north part vpon Scotland, and vpon the south side, it respecteth Germanie. And is inhabited with thrée sundrie sortes of people, Englishmen, Cornishmen, and welchmen, all which if not in lawes, and constitutions, yet in language doe differ one from another. But as they doe differ in tong, and spéech, so are they subiect (and that Patrio iure, By iustice, & law)

B. 4. to

to one Prince, and gouernour onely to whom
they owe their allegeance.

Theod.   Is the country quiet, peaceable,
and at vnitie within it selfe, or otherwise tro-
bled with matenies, wars, and ciuill dissen-
tions?

Amphil.   The whole lande (God be praised
therefore, and preserue hir noble Grace by
whom it is gouerned, and maintained) is, and
hath beene at peace, and vnitie not onely within it selfe, but also abroad for this foure or fiue
and twenty yeeres. During all which time
there hath beene neither wars, inuasions, in-
surrections, nor any effusion of blood to speake
of, except of a sort of archtraitours, who haue
receiued but the same reward they deserued,
and the same that I pray God all traitours
with their complices may receiue hereafter, if
they practise the same, which they haue done.
The like continuance of peace was neuer
heard of not this hundred yeeres before, as this
country hath inioied since hir maiesties reigne
the Lord preserue hir grace, and roiall Maiestie for euer.

Theod.   Are the other countries, lands,
and nations about them (for as I gather by
your former intimations this country is
scituate as it were in the centrie, or midst of
gthers)

others) their friends, and welwillers, or their enimies?

Amphil. It is an old saieng and true : Ex incertis, & ambiguis rebus optimū tenere ſapientis eſt: Of things vncerteine a chriſtian man ought to iudge, and hope the beſt. They hope wel that all are their friends and welwillers: but it is thought (and I feare me to true) that they are ſo far from being their friends (Niſi verbo tenus, from mouth outward onely) that they haue vowed and ſworne their deſtruction, if they could as eaſily atchiue it, as they ſecretly intend it. Which thing to be true, ſome of their late practiſes haue (yet to their owne confuſion, Gods name be praiſed) proued true. For how manie times hath that man of ſinne, that ſonne of the diuell, that Italian Antichriſt of Rome interdicted, excommunicated, ſuſpended, and accurſed with boke, bell, and candle, both the Prince, the Nobilitie, the Commons, and whole Realme? How often hath he ſent forth his roring buls againſt hir Maieſtie, excommunicating (as I haue ſaid) hir Grace, and diſcharging hir Highneſſe liege people, and naturall ſubiects from their alleageance to hir Grace? How often hath he with his adherents conſpired and intended the death and ouerthrowe of hir Maieſtie, and Nobilitie by coniuration,

juration, necromancy, exorcismes, art magike,
witchcraft, and all kind of diuelrie besides,
wherein the most part of them are skilfuller,
than in diuinitie? And when these deuises
would not take place, nor effect as they wished, then attempted they by other waies and
meanes to ouerthrowe the estate, the Prince,
nobles, people, and country: sometime by secret irruption, sometime by open inuasion, in-
surrection, and rebellion, sometime by open
treason, sometime by secret conspiracie, and
sometimes by one meanes, sometimes by another. And now of late attempted they the ouerthrowe and subuersion of hir Maiestie, people,
country, and all, by sending into the realme a
sort of cutthrotes, false traitors, and bloudthir-
stie Papists, who vnder the pretence of religious men (in whom for the most part there is
as much religion as is in a dog) should not
onely lurke in corners like howlets that ab-
horre the light, crepe into noble mens bosoms,
thereby to withdrawe hir Maiesties subiects
from their allegeance, but also moue them to
rebellion, and to take sword in hand against
Prince, country, yea and against God himselfe
(if it were possible) and to dispense with them
that shall thus mischieuouslye behaue themselues. And forsooth these goodlie fellowes, the
diuels

diuels agents, that muſt woꝛke theſe feates, are called (in the diuels name) by the name of Ieſuites, ſeminarie pꝛeſts, and catholikes, vſurping to themſelues a name neuer heard of till of late daies, being indæd a name verie blaſphemouſly deriued from the name of Ieſus, and impꝛoperly alluded and attributed to themſelues. But what will it pꝛeuaile them to be like vnto Ieſus in name onely, oꝛ how can they, nay how dare they arrogate that name vnto themſelues, wheras their doctrine, religion, and whole pꝛofeſſion, togither with their coꝛrupt liues and conuerſations are direaly contrarie to the doctrine, religion, life, and pꝛofeſſion of Chꝛiſt Ieſus ? There is nothing in the woꝛld moꝛe contradictoꝛie one to another, than all their pꝛocædings in generall are to Chꝛiſt Ieſus, and his lawes, and yet will they vnder the pꝛetence of a bare and naked name, pꝛomiſe to themſelues ſuch excellencie, ſuch integritie, and perfection, as GOD cannot require moꝛe, yea ſuch as doth merite Ex opere operato, Eternall felicitie in the heauens. And thus they deceiue themſelues, and delude the woꝛld alſo with their traſh : but of them inough.

Theod. Surely that country had næde to take hæd to it ſelfe, to feare, and ſtand in awe,

hauing

hauing so manie enimies on euerie side. And
aboue all things next vnto the seruing of God,
to kéepe themselues aloofe, and in any case not
to trust them what faire weather soeuer they
make them : but rather to thinke thus, that
when they flatter them the most, then intend
they the most mischiefe against them. The
swéeter the Syren singeth, the dangerouser is
it to lend hir our eares : the Cocatrice neuer
meaneth so much crueltie, as when he faw-
neth vpon thée, and wéepeth, then take héed, for
he meaneth to sucke thy bloud. The stiller the
water standeth, the more perilous it is. Let
them remember it is an old and true saieng :
Sub melle iacet venenum, Under hony lieth hid
poison. Sub placidis herbis latitat coluber, vnder
the pleasantest grasse, lurketh the venemoust
adder. Take héed of those fellowes that haue
Mel in ore, verba lactis, swéet words, and plausible spéeches : for they haue Fel in corde, and
Fraudem factis, Gall in their harts, & deceit in
their deeds. So falleth it out with these ambi-
dexters, these hollowe harted friends, where
they intend destruction, then will they couer it
with the cloke or garment of amity & friend-
ship, therefore are they not to be trusted.

Amphil. You say the truth. For I am thus
persuaded, that he who is false to God (as all
Papists

Papists with their complices and adherents are) can neuer be true and faithfull, neither to prince nor country. Therefore God grant they may be taken héed of betimes.

Theod. Considering that this country of Dnalgne is enuied abroad with so many enimies, and infested within by so many seditions Papists, and hollowe harted people, it is great maruell, that it can stand without great wars, and troubles. Belike it hath a wise politike prince, and good gouernors, either else it were vnpossible to preserue the same in such peace and tranquillitie, and that so long togither. I pray you therefore by what prince is the same gouerned, and after what maner?

Amphil. The whole realme or country of Dnalgne is ruled, and gouerned by a noble Quéene, a chaste Maide, and pure Virgin, who for all respects may compare with any vnder the sunne. In so much as I doubt not to call hir sacred breast the promptuarie, the receptacle, or storehouse of all true virtue and godlines. For if you speake of wisdome, knowledge and vnderstanding, hir Grace is singular, yea, able at the first blush, to discearne truth from falsehood, and falsehood from truth in any matter, how ambiguous or obscure soeuer: so as it may iustly be called into question whether

Salomon

Salomon himselfe had greater light of wisedome instilled into his sacred breast, then hir
maiestie hath into hir highnes roiall minde. If
you speake of learning and knowledge in the
toongs, whether it be in the Latine, Græke,
French, Dutch, Italian, Spanish, or any other
vsuall toong, it may be doubted whether Chri-
stendome hath hir pǽre, or not. If you speake
of sobrietie, modestie, mansuetude, and gentlenesse, it is woonderfull in hir Highnesse,
yea, so affable, so lowly and humble is hir
Grace, as she will not disdaine to talke famili-
arlie to the meanest, or porest of hir Graces
subiects vpon speciall occasions. If you speake
of mercie, and compassion to euery one that
hath offended, I stande in suspence whether hir
like were euer borne. If you speake of religion, of zeale and feruencie to the truth, or if
you speake of the vpright execution or administration of iustice, all the world can beare wit-
nes, that herein (as in all godlinesse else) hir
Highnes is inferior to none that liueth at this
day. So that hir Grace sǽmeth rather a diuine creature, then an earthly creature, a ves-
sel of grace, mercie, and compassion, whereinto
the Lord hath powred euen the full measures
of his superabundant grace, and heauenlie influence. The Lord increase the same in hir
Highnes

Highnes roiall breast, and preserue hir Grace, to the end of the world, to the glorie of God, the comfort of hir Maiesties subiects, and confusion of all hir enimies whatsoeuer.

Theod. What is hir Maiesties Councell? It should séeme that they must néedes be excellent men, hauing such a vertuous Ladie and Phenix Quéene to rule ouer them?

Amphil. The Councell are Honorable and noble personages indéed, of great grauitie, wisedome, and pollicie, of singular experience, modestie and discretion, for zeale to religion famous, for dexteritie in giuing counsell renoumed, for the administration of iustice, incomparable, finally, for all honorable and noble exploits inferior to none, or rather excelling all. So as their worthie déedes through the golden trumpe of fame are blowne ouer all the worlde. The whole regiment of the Realme consisteth in the execution of god lawes, sanctions, statutes, and constitutions enacted and set forth by hir royall Maiestie, and hir most honorable Councel, and committed by the same to inferior officers, and maiestrates to be put in practise, by whose diligent execution thereof, iustice is maintained, vertue erected, iniurie repressed, and sinne seuerely punished, to the great glorie of God, and

common

common tranquilitie of the Realme in euery condition.

Theod. Is the lande diuided into shires, counties, precincts, and seuerall exempt liberties, to the ende iustice may the better be maintained? And hath euery county, shire, and precinct, good lawes in the same for the deciding, and appealing of controuersies that happen in the same, so that they neede not to seeke further for redresse than in their owne shire?

Amphil. The whole land indeede is diuided (as you say, into shires, counties, and seuerall precincts, (which are in number as I take it 40. In euerie which shire or countie be courts, lawe dayes, and leets, as they call them, euery moneth, or euery quarter of a yeare, wherin any controuersie (lightlie) may be heard and determined, so that none needs (except vpon some speciall occasions) to seeke to other courts for deciding of any controuersie. But as there be good lawes if they were executed dulie, so are there corruptions, and abuses, not a few crept into them. For sometimes you shall haue a matter hang in sute after it is commenced a quarter of a yeare, halfe a yeare, yea, a twelue month, two or three yeeres togither, yea, seauen or eight yeeres now and then, if either friends or money can

be

be made. This deferring of iustice is as damnable before God, as the sentence of false iudgment is, as that blessed martyr of God Maister
Latimer hath said in a sermon made before
King Edward the sirt. Besides this deferring
and delaieng of poore mens causes, I will not
say how iudgement is peruerted in the end. I
read them take heed to it that be the authors
thereof. Therefore the reformed churches beyond the seas are worthie of commendations,
for there the Iudges sit in the open gates,
streets, and high waies, that euery man that
will may speake vnto them, and complaine if
he haue occasion. And so farre from delaieng,
or putting of poore mens causes be they, as
they will not suffer any matter how weightie
soeuer to hang in sute aboue one day, or two,
or at the most three daies, which happeneth
verie seldome. But if the lawes within euery
particular countie or shire were duly admini-
stred without parcialitie, and truly executed
with all expedition, as they ought, and not so
lingred as they be, then needed not the poore
people to run 100.200,yea 300.or 400.miles
(as commonly they doe) to seeke iustice, when
they might haue it nearer home : through the
want whereof,besides that their sutes are like
to hang in ballance peraduenture seuen yeares,

C. I.   they

they hauing spent al in the end fall to extreme beggerie, which inconuenience might easilie be remoued, if all matters, and causes whatsoeuer were heard at home in their owne shire, or countie with expedition. And to say the truth, what fooles are they (yea woorthie to be inaugured fooles with the laurell crowne of triple follie) that whilst they might haue iustice at home in their owne country, and all matters of controuersie decided amongst their neighbors and friends at home, will yet go to lawe two or three hundred miles distant from them, and spend all that they haue to inrich a sort of greedie lawiers, when at the last a sort of ignorant men of their neighbors must make an end of it whether they will or not. This me thinke, if euerie good man would perpend in himselfe, he would neither go to lawe himself, nor yet giue occasion to others to doe the like.

Theod. I gather by your speeches that these people are very contentious and quarellous, either else they would neuer be so desirous of reuenge, nor yet prosecute the lawe so seuerely for euery trifle.

Amphil. They are very contentious indeed. Insomuch as if one giue neuer so small occasion to another, sute must straight be commensed, and to lawe go they as round as a ball, till
either

either both, or at least the one become a begger all daies of his life after.

Theod. But on the other side, if they shuld not go to lawe, then should they suftaine great wrong, and be iniuried on euery side.

Amphl. Indeed the lawe was made for the administration of equitie and iustice, for the appeasing of controuersies & debates, and for to giue to euery man (Quod suum est) That which is his owne, but being now peruerted & abused to cleane contrarie ends (for now commonly the law is ended as a man is frinded) is it not better to suffer a little wrong with patience, referring the reuenge to him who saith: Mihi vindictam, & ego retribuam, Uengeance is mine, and I wil reward, than for a trifle to go to lawe, and spende all that euer he hath, and yet come by no remedie neither? Our sauiour Christ biddeth vs if any man will go to law with vs for our cote, to giue him our cloke also, and if any man will giue thee a blowe on the one cheeke, turne to him the other, whereby is ment, that if any man will iniurie vs, and doe vs wrong, we should not resiff, nor trouble our selues, but suffer awhile, and with patience refer the due reuenge thereof to the Lord.

Amphil. Why? Is it not lawful then for one
C. 2.   Christian

Chzistian man, to go to lawe with another?

Amphil. The Apostle saith many things are lawfull which are not expedient, and therfore although it be after a sort lawfull, yet for euery trifle it is not lawfull, but for matters of importance it is. And yet not neither, if the matter might otherwise by neighbors at home be determined.

Theod. Yet some doubt whether it be lawfull or no for one Chzistian man to go to lawe with another for any worldly matter, bringing in the apostle Paule rebuking the Corinthians for going to lawe one with another.

Amphil. The apostle in that place reprehendeth them not for going to lawe for reasonable causes, but for that they being chzistians went to lawe vnder heathen iudges, which tended to the great discredite, and infamie of the Gospell. But certeine it is though some Anabaptists Quibus veritas odio est, and certeine other heritikes haue taught the contrarie, yet it is certeine, that one chzistian man may go to law with another for causes reasonable. For it being true as it cannot be denied, that there is a certeine singularitie, interest, and propzietie in every thing, and the lawe being not onely the meane to conserue the same propziety, but also to restore it againe
being

being violate is therefoze lawfull, and may
lawfully be attempted out, yet with this pzo-
uiſo, that it is better, if the matter may otherwiſe be apeaſed at home, not to attempt lawe,
than to attempt it. But if any ſchiſmatikes (as
alas the wozlde is too full of them) ſhould altogither deny the vſe of the lawe, as not chziſtian, beſides that the manifeſt wozd of God in
euery place would eaſilie conuince them, the
examples, and pzactiſes of all ages, times,
countries and nations,from the firſt beginning
of the wozld,togither with the example of our
ſauiour Chziſt himſelfe, who ſubmitted himſelf to the lawes then eſtabliſhed,would quick-
lie ouerthzow their vaine imaginations. The
lawe in it ſelfe, is the ſquare, the leuell, and
rule of equitie,and inſtice, and therefoze who
abſolutely contendeth the ſame not to be chziſtian, may well be accuſed of extréme folly.
But if the lawes be wicked and antichziſtian,
then ought not good chziſtians to ſue vnto thé,
but rather to ſuſtaine all kind of wzong whatſoeuer.

  Theod. Then it ſéemeth by your reaſon,
that if the lawe be ſo neceſſarie,as without the
which Chziſtian kingdomes could not ſtand,
then are lawiers neceſſarie alſo foz the execution thereof.

Amphil. They are most necessarie. And in my iudgement a man can serue God, in no calling better, than in it, if he be a man of a good conscience, but in Dnalgne the lawiers haue such chancerell consciences, that they can serue the deuill better in no kind of calling than in that: for they handle poore mens matters coldly, they execute iustice parcially, & they receiue bribes gréedily, so that iustice is peruerted, the poore beggered, and many a good man iniuried therby. They respect the persons, and not the causes, mony, not the poore, rewards, and not conscience. So that law is turned almost topsie turuie, and therefore happie is he, that hath least to doe with them.

Theod. The lawiers must néedes be verie rich if they haue such large consciences.

Amphil. Rich quoth you? They are rich indéede toward the deuill, and the world, but towards God and heauen, they are poore inough. It is no meruaile if they be rich and get much when they wil not speak two words vnder an angell (for that is called a councellers fée.) But how they handle the poore mens causes for it, God and their owne consciences can tell, and one day I feare me, they shall féele to their perpetuall paine, except they repent and amend.

Theod.

Theod. How be judgements executed there vpon offenders, transgressours, and malefactors, with equitie, & expedition, or otherwise.

Amphil. It greeueth me to relate thereof vnto you, the abuses therein are so inormous: For if a felone, homicide, a murtherer, or else what greeuous offender soeuer, that hath deserued a thousand deaths, if it were possible, happen to be taken and apprehended, he is straightway committed to prison, and clapt vp in as many cold yrons as he can beare, yea, throwne into dungeons, and darke places vnder the ground, without either bed, clothes, or any thing else to helpe himselfe withall, saue a little straw or litter bad inough for a dog to lie in. And in this miserie shall he lie amongst frogs, toades, and other filthie vermine, till lice eate the flesh of his bones. In the meane space hauing nothing to eate, but either bread and water, or else some other modicum scarce able to suffice nature, and many times it happeneth, that for want of the same pittance they are macerate and shronke so low, as they either looke like ghosts, or else are famished out of hand. And this extreeme misery they lie in sometime (perhaps) a quarter of a yeere, sometimes halfe a yeere, a tweluemonth, yea, sometimes two or three yeeres, and perchance

G.4　　　　all

all their life though they haue deserued death,
by their flagitious facts committed. Who seeth
not that it were much better for them to die at
once, than to suffer this extreeme miserie? Yea
the sufferance of this extremitie is better vnto
them, than the tast of present death it selfe. And
therefore in the cities reformed beyond seas,
there is notable order for this: for as soone any
fellon or malefactor whatsoeuer, that hath deserued death is taken, he is brought before the
magistrate, witnesse comes in, and giues eui-
dence against him, and being found gilty, and
conuict by iustice, is presently without any
farther imprisonment, repriuation or delay,
condemned, and being condemned, is led presently to the place of execution, and so committed to the sword.

Theod. What is the cause why they are
kept so long before they go to execution in
Dnalgne.

Amphil. Sometimes it commeth to passe
by reason of (will doe all) otherwise called
mony, and sometimes by freends, or both, for
certeine it is, the one will not worke without
the other. Hereby it commeth to passe, that
great abuses are committed. For if any man
that hath freends and mony (as mony alwaies
bringeth freendes with him) chance to haue
                                                    commit-

committed neuer so heinous, or flagicious a
dæd, whether robbed, stollen, slaine, killed, or
murthered, or whatsoeuer it be, then letters
walke, frænds bestir them, and mony carieth
all away: yea, and though the lawe condemns
him, iustice conuicteth him, and good conscience
executeth him, yet must he nædes be repriued,
and in the meane time his pardon by false sug-
gestion forsœth must be purchased, either for
frændship or mony.

Theod. That is a great abuse, that he
whom the lawe of God and of man doth condemne, should be pardoned. Can man pardon
or remit him, whom God doth condemne? Or
shall man be more mercifull in euill, then the
author of mercie himselfe, it is God that con-
demneth, who is he that can saue? Therefore
those that ought to die by the lawe of God, are
not to be saued by the lawe of man. The lawe
of God commandeth that the murtherer, the
adulterer, the exorcist, magician, and witch,
and the like, should die the death. Is it now in
the power or strength of man to pardon him
his life?

Amphil. Although it be wilfull and purpo-
sed murther, yet is the prince borne in hande
that it was plaine chance medley (as they call
it) mære casuall, and fortunate, and therefore
may

may eaſily be diſpenſed withall. Indœde the wiſedome of God ordeined, that if any man chanced to kill an other againſt his will, he ſhould flie to certeine cities of refuge, and ſo be ſaued, but if it were proued that he killed him wittingly, willingly, & prepenſedly, then he ſhould without al exception be put to death. And herein is great abuſe, that two hauing committed one and the ſame fault the one ſhal be pardoned, and the other executed. If it be ſo that both haue committed offence worthy of death, let both die for it, if not, why ſhould either die. Experience proueth this true, for if a Gentleman commit a grieuous offence, and a poore man commit the like, the poore ſhal be ſure of his Surſum collum? But the other ſhall be pardoned. So Diogenes ſœing a ſort of poore men going to hanging fell into a great laughter. And being demanded wherefore he laughed, he anſwered at the vanitie, and follie of this blind word. For ſaith he, I ſœe great thœues lead little thœues to hanging. And to ſay the truth, before God, is not he a greater thœfe that robbeth a man of his good name for euer, that taketh a mans houſe ouer his head, before his yeres be expired, that wreſteth frō a man his goods, his lands, and liuings, wher-vpon he, his wiſe, children and familie ſhould
liue,

line, than he that stealeth a sheepe, a cow, or an oxe, for necessities sake onely, hauing not otherwise to releeue his neede? And is not he a great theefe that taketh great summes of mony of the poore (vnder the names of fees, and doth litle or nothing for them? Though this be not theft before the world, nor punishable by penall lawes, yet before God it is plaine theft, and punishable with eternall torments in hel. Let them take heede to it.

Theod. Cannot the prince then pardon any malefactor?

Amphil. Some are of opinion that the prince by his power imperiall and prorogatiue may pardon and remit the penaltie of any law, either diuine, or humane, but I am of opinió that if Gods law condemne him, no prince ought to saue him, but to execute iudgement, and iustice without respect of persons to all indifferently. But in causes wherin Gods lawe doth not condemne him, the prince may pardon the offender, if there appeere likelyhoode of amendment in him. And yet let the prince be sure of this, to answere at the day of iudgment before the tribunall seate of GOD, for all the offences that the partie pardoned shall commit any time of his life after. For if the prince had cutte him off when the

lawe

lawe had passed on him, that euill had not bæen
committed. To this purpose I remember I
haue heard a certeine prettie apothegue vttered by a iester to a king. The king had pardoned one of his subiectes that had committed
murther, who being pardoned committed the
like offence againe, and by meanes was pardoned the second time also, and yet filling vp
the measure of his iniquitie, killed the third,
and being brought before the king, the king
being very sorie, asked why he had killed
thræ men, to whom his iester standing by
replied, saieng: No (O king) he killed but
the first, and thou hast killed the other two: for
if thou hadst hanged him vp at the first, the o-
ther two had not bæne killed, therefore thou
hast killed them, and shalt answere for their
bloud. Which thing being heard, the king hanged him vp straightway as he very well deserued: yet notwithstanding I grant that a prince
by his power regall, and prerogatiue imperial
may pardon offenders, but not such as Gods
lawes and good conscience doe condemne, as I
said before. The power of a prince is compre-
hended In Rebus licitis in Deo, but not In Rebus illicitis contra Deum : In things lawfull
in God, not in things vnlawfull contrarie to
God. No power or principalitie vpon the earth
whatsoeuer

whatsoeuer may dispense with the lawe of God, but what it setteth downe must stand inuiolable. Therefore if it be asked me wherein a prince may pardon any malefactor, I answer for the breach or violation of any humane lawe, ordinance, constitution, statute, or sanction, but not against Gods word and lawe in any condition.

Theod. How is iustice ministred there, sincerely and truely, so as the poore haue no cause iustly to complaine, or otherwise?

Amphil. If any haue cause to complaine (as alas too many haue) it is for want of due execution of the lawes, not for lacke of good lawes. For God be praised there be many good lawes, but indeed now and then through the negligence of the officers they are coldly executed. But if the lawes there in force were without parcialitie dulie executed, there sholo be no iust occasion for any to complaine. And truly to speake my conscience there is great parcialitie in the magistrates and officers, nay great corruption. For if a rich man, and a poore man chance to haue to doe before them, the matter I warrant you shall quickly be ended, and my life for yours shall go vpon the rich mans side, notwithstanding the poore mans right be apparent to all the world. But

if

if two poꝛe men of equall eſtate go to lawe togither, then their ſute ſhall hang thꝛꝛ oꝛ foure
yæres, peraduenture ſeuen yæres, a doȝen, yea
twentie yæres befoꝛe it be ended, till either
the one, oꝛ both be made beggers. Foꝛ refoꝛma-
tion whereof I would wiſh iudges and officers to reſpect the cauſe, not the perſons, the
matter, not the gaine: and not to regard either
letter oꝛ any thing elſe, which might be ſent
them to peruert true iudgement. And iuſtice
being miniſtred, then to read ouer their com-
mendatoꝛie letters in Gods name, remem-
bꝛing what the wiſe man ſaith : Gifts blinde
the eies of the wiſe, and peruert iudgement.
The lawiers I would wiſh to take leſſe fæs of
their clients. Foꝛ is not this a plaine theft befoꝛe God to take ten, twentie, oꝛ foꝛtie ſhil-
liñgs of one poꝛe man at one time, and ſo
much of a great ſoꝛt at once, and yet to ſpeake
neuer a woꝛd foꝛ the moſt part of it? And notwithſtanding that they can be preſent but at
one barre at once ; yet will they take diuers
fæs of ſundꝛy clients to ſpeake foꝛ them at
thꝛꝛ oꝛ foure places in one day. The other officers who grant foꝛth the warrants, the Sub
pœnas, the Scire facias, and diuers other wꝛits,
and thoſe who kæpe the ſeales of the ſame, I
would wiſh to take leſſe fæs alſo. Foꝛ is not
this

this too vnreaſonable to take a crowne, or ten ſhillings for wꝛiting ſix oꝛ ſeuen lines, oꝛ little moꝛe. And then the keeper of the ſeale, foꝛ a little ware, he muſt haue as much as the other. And thus they ſucke out (as it were) euen the very marrowe ont of pooꝛe mens bones. The ſhirifs, bailifs, and other officers alſo, I would wiſh, foꝛ fees, foꝛ bꝛibes, foꝛ friendſhip and rewards, not to returne a Tarde venit, oꝛ a Non eſt inuentus, when they either haue ſent the partie woꝛd to avoid couertly, oꝛ elſe looking thꝛough their fingers ſee him, & wil not ſee him, foꝛcing herby the pooꝛe plaintife to loſe not onely his great & impoꝛtable charges in the lawe, bot alſo peraduenture his whole right of that which he ſueth foꝛ. Thus let euery officer by what kind of name oꝛ title ſoeuer he be called, oꝛ in what kind of calling ſoeuer he be placed, doe all things with ſingle eie, and good conſcience, that God may be gloꝛified, the common peace maintained, iuſtice ſuppoꝛted, and their owne conſciences diſcharged againſt the great daye of the Loꝛde, when all fleſh ſhall be conuented befoꝛe the tribunall ſeate of G O D all naked as euer they were boꝛne, to render accounts of all their dooings, whether they bee good oꝛ badde, and to receiue a rewarde accoꝛding to their deeds.

By

By all which it appeareth that if any for want of iustice haue cause to complaine, it is thorow the corruption of iniquitie, auarice, and ambition of greedy and insaciable cormorants, who for desire of gaine, make hauocke of all things, yea, make shipwracke of bodies and soules to the deuill for euer, vnlesse they repent.

Theod. How farre are princes lawes to be obeied, in all things indifferently without exception?

Amphil. In all things not contrarie to the lawe of God and good conscience, which if they be against God, and true godlinesse, then must we say with the apostles, Melius est deo obedire, quam hominibus, It is better to obey God than man.

Theod. If the prince than doe set forth a lawe contrarie to the lawe of God, and do constraine vs to doe that, that Gods words commandeth vs we shall not doe. In this or the like case, may subiects lawfully take armes, and rise against their prince?

Amphil. No, at no hand, vnlesse they will purchase to themselues eternall damnation, and the wrath of God for euer. For it is not lawfull for the subiects to rise vp in armes against their liege prince for any occasion whatsoeuer,

soeuer. For proofe whereof we read that our sauiour Christ was, not onely obedient to the maigistrates, and superior powers in all things, but also taught his apostles, disciples, and in them all people and nations of the world, the very same doctrine. And therefore the apostle saith, Omnis anima potestatibus superioribus subdita sit? Let euery soule submit himselfe to the higher powers, for there is no power but of God. And he that resisteth this power, resisteth the ordinance of God, and purchaseth to himselfe eternall damnation. Peter also giueth the like charge, that obedience in all godlines be giuen to the superior powers, and that praiers and intercessions be made, for kings and rulers, and giueth the reason why, namely, that we may lead Vitam pacificam, A peaceable life vnder them.

Theod. Why? How then? If we shall not resist them, then we do obey them in any thing either good, or bad.

Amphil. No, not so neither. In all things not contrarie to Gods word we must obey the͂, on paine of damnation. But in things contrarie to the word and truth of God, we are thus to doe. We must depose and lay forth our selues both bodie, and goods, life, and lime, (our

conscience

conscience onely excepted, in the true obedience whereof, we are to serue our God) euen
all that we haue of nature, and committing
the same into the hands of the prince, submit
our selues, and lay downe our necks vpon the
blocke, choosing rather to die than to doe any
thing contrarie to the lawe of God and good
conscience. And this is that, that the apostles
ment when they saide : It is better to obey
God than man. Not that obedience to man in
all godlinesse is forbid, but that obedience to
God is to be preferred before the obedience to
man.

Theod. What if the prince be a tyrant, a
wicked prince, and an vngodly, is he notwithstanding to be obeied?

Amphil. Yea truely in the same order as
I haue shewed before. For whether the
prince be wicked, or godlye, hee is sent of
GOD, bicause the Apostle saith : There is
no power but of GOD. If the prince be
a godlye prince, then is hee sent as a great
blessing from GOD, and if hee be a tyrant,
then is he raised of GOD for a scourge to
the people for their sinnes . And therefore
whether the prince be the one, or the other, he
is to be obeied as before.

Theod. And bee kings and rulers to
bee

bee beloued, and praied for of their subiects?

Amphil. That is without all doubt. For
hee that hateth his prince in his hart, is a
contemner of Gods ordinance, a traitour vnto GOD, and to his countreye: yea hee
is to loue his prince as well as himselfe,
and better, if better can bee, and to praye
for him as for himselfe. For that an infinite number doe rest and depend vppon his
Maiestie, which doe not so vppon himselfe.
So that the miscarrieng of him, were the
destruction (peraduenture) of manye thou-
sands.

Theod. This being so, then hath Dnalgne great cause to praye for their prince, by
whose woorthye indeuour, and wise gouernement, the state of that realme is so peaceably
maintained.

Amphil. They haue great cause indeede
not onely to loue hir Maiestie, but also to
praye for hir Grace, and whosoeuer will
not doe so, I beseech the LORDE in the
bowels of his mercie, to stoppe their breath,
and to take them awaye quicklye from the
face of the earth. For by hir Highnesse
wise gouernement, the realme is in peace,
Gods worde flourisheth, and aboundance

of al things floweth in the same, the Lord God be praised therefore, and preserue hir noble Grace long to reigne amongst vs. Amen.

Theod. Let vs proceed a little further, I pray you how is the youth of that country brought vp in learning, or otherwise?

Amphil. The youth truely is well brought vp, both in good letters, nurture, and maners for the most part. For the better performance whereof, they haue excellent good schooles, both in cities, townes, and countries, wherin abundance of children are learnedly brought vp, But yet notwithstanding some parents are much to be blamed in the education of their children, for the most kéepe their sonnes to schoole, but for a time, till they can write and read, and well if all that too, and very seldome or neuer doe they kéepe them so long at their bookes, as vntill they atteine to any perfect knowledge indéed. So that by this means learning doth and is like greatly to decay. And if one aske them, why they kéepe not their children to schoole till they proue learned, they h... answer, Bicause I sée learning and learned men are little estéemed, and me thinke the best of them can hardly liue by the same. And therefore I will set him to an occupation, which will be alwaies sure. As herein they say true,

true, so I cannot but lament the small preferment now adaies that learning getteth in the world amongst men, & the smal account that is made of the same. This is the cause why learning doth, and will in time greatly decay. For who is he that hauing spent all his substance vpon learning, yea his bodie, strength, and all, and yet can hardly liue thereby, and maintaine himselfe withall, that will couet after learning, which is both so chargeable, and painfull to be come by?

Theod. Be there not Uniuersities, colledges, and free schooles, where youth may bee brought vp in learning Gratis without any charges to their parents?

Amphil. There are such places indeed. But alas they are abused & peruerted to other ends than was intended by them at the first. For whereas those places had great liuings, rents, reuenues, & possessions giuen to them, it was to this onely end and purpose, that those poore children whose parents were not able otherwise to maintaine them at learning, should be brought vp vpon the charges of the house, and not those whose parents are able to maintaine them of themselues. But now we see the contrarie is true, and whereas they were giuen to maintaine none but the poore only, now

they

they maintaine none but the rich onely. For
except one be able to giue the regent or prouost
of the house, a pæce of mony, ten pound, twentie pound, fortie pound, yea, a hundred pound,
a yoke of fatte oxen, or a couple of fine gel-
dings, or the like though he be neuer so toward
a youth, nor haue neuer so much næd of maintenance, yet he comes not there I warant him.
If he canot preuaile this way. Let him get him
letters comendatory from some of reputation,
and perchance he may spæd, in hope of benefite
to insue. So that the places in the vniuersities
and fræ scholes, sæme rather to be solde for
mony and frienship, then giuen gratis, to them
that haue næde, as they ought to be.

Theod. Are there not many inferior scholes
in the country besides, both for the instruction
and catechising of youth?

Amhpil. There are so, almost in euery parish. But alas, such small pittance is allowed
the scholmaisters, as they can neither buy the
libraries, nor which is lesse, hardly maintaine
themselues, which thing altogither disuadeth
them from their bookes, and is occasion why
many a one snorteth in palpable ignorance all
daies of their life.

Theod. Would you haue any man without
exception, to take vppon him the office of a
schol

schoolmaister, and to teach the youth?

Amphil. No at no hand. First I would wish
that euery one that is a schoolmaister, how learned, or vnlearned soeuer, should be examined,
as wel for his religion, and his sufficiencie in
knowledge, as also for his integritie of life, &
being found sound in them all, to be alowed &
admitted to teach. For if euerie one that wold
should take vpon him to teach without further
triall, then might there great inconuenience
follow. For papists and other schismatikes, a-
postataes, or else whatsoeuer, might thrust in
themselues, & so corrupt the youth. Ignorant &
vnlearned would take vpon them high learning, & so delude their schoolers. And if his life
should not be answerable to his profession, then
should he peruert his auditorie also. Therefore
in my iudgement is there great choise to be
made of schoolmaisters. Thus they being tried,
let them be admitted gratis, by authoritie. But
now there is great abuses herein, for being
found sufficient in all respects, yet must he be
constrained to take a license, whether he will
or not, and must pay x.xvi.or xx.shillings for it
& yet will this serue him no longer, than he ta-
rieth in that dioces, & comming into another he
must pay as much there for y like license also,
whereas peraduenture he shall scarcely get so

D.4.   much

much cléere in thrée or foure yéeres, in that dioces, they haue such fat pasture. But if they would néedes haue them to haue licenses, (which I grant to be very good.) I would wish they might haue them gratis, without mony, for if it be lawfull for them to teach for mony, it is also lawfull without. And if they be not worthie, it is pittie that mony should make them worthie, and againe, if they be worthie, it is pittie that without mony they cannot be so accepted.

Theod. What way were best to be taken for the good education of youth?

Amphil. It were good (if it might be brought to passe) that in euery parish throughout the Realme, there were an indifferent able man appointed for the instruction of youth in good letters, hauing a reasonable stipend alowed him of the same parish for his paines. But now they teach and take paines, for little or nothing, which vtterly discourageth them, and maketh manie a colde schooler, in Dnalgne, as experience daily teacheth.

Theod. Be there men of all kinde of trades, occupations, and artes, as there be in other countries.

Amhpil. Yea, truely: there are men of all sciences, trades, mysteries, faculties, occupations

tions, and artes whatſoeuer, and that as cunning as any be vnder the ſunne. Yea, ſo expert
they be, as if they would let a thing alone whē
it is well, they were the brauest workmen in
the world. But as they ſæke to excell and ſur-
paſſe al other nations, in fineneſſe of workman-
ſhip, ſo now and than they reape the fruits of
their vaine curioſity, to their owne detriment,
hinderance, and decay.

Theod. How liue the marchant men a-
mongſt them, are they rich and wealthy, or
but poore?

Amphil. How ſhould they be poore, gaining as they do, more then halfe in halfe in euerie thing they buy or ſell? And which is more,
ſometimes they gaine double and triple, if I
ſaid quadruple I lied not.

Theod. I pray you how can that be ſo?

Amphil. I will tell you. They haue mony
to lay forth vpon euerie thing, to buy them at
the firſt, and beſt hand, yea, to ingroſſe, and to
ſtore themſelues with abundance of al things.
And then will they keepe theſe marchandize
till they waxe verie ſcarſe; (and no maruaile
for they buy vp all things) and ſo conſequently dære. And then will they ſell them at their
owne prices, or elſe (being able to beare the
mony) they will keepe them ſtill.   By this
meanes

they get the deuill and all, besides these, they
haue a hundzed flights in their budgets to rake
in gaine withall.

Theod. I pzay you what be those?

Amphil. They will go into the countries,
and buy vp all the wooll, cozne, leather, butter
cheese, bacon, oz else what marchandize soeuer
they knowe will be vendible, and these they
transpozt ouer seas, whereby they gaine infini
summes of mony.

Theod. That is woonderfull that they
are so permitted: are there no lawes, noz
pzohibitions to the contrarie, that no wooll,
cozne, oz leather, shoulde be transpozted ouer
seas?

Amphil. There are good lawes, and grea
restraints to the contrary, in so much as they
be apparent traitoz to God, their pzince and
country, that carrie any of the fozesaid thing
ouer without speciall licence thereto. Yet not
withstanding, either by hooke, oz crooke, by
night oz day, by direct, oz indirect meanes, ei
ther knowne oz vnknowne, they wil conueigh
them ouer, though their owne country want
the same. But to auoide all dangers, they puz
chase a licence, & a dispensation foz mony, bea
ring the pzince in hand that they do it foz some
good cause, when indeed the cause is their owne
pziuate

pziuate gaine. And foz the ſpeedier obtaining of
their deſires , they demand licence foz the ca-
riage ouer but of ſo much and ſo much, when
in truth they conuey ouer vnder the colour
of this their licence ten times, twenty times,
yea, a hundzed times, fiue hundzed times,
yea, a thouſande times as much moze. And
thus they delude their pzince , impoueriſh
their country, and inrich themſelues, feeding,
clothing and inriching our enimies with our
owne treaſure. Hereby it commeth to paſſe
that all things are deerer, and ſcarſer, than o-
therwiſe they would be, if reſtraynt were
had, and J warrant them many a blacke curſe
haue they of the pooze commons foz their doing.

Theod. Would you not haue licences
granted foz the tranſpozting ouer of ſuch
things foz no cauſe?

Amphil.   Yes . But firſt J would haue
our owne people ſerued that they wante
not in any caſe . Foz it is very vnmeete to
feede fozren nations, and our owne country fa-
miſh at home. But if it were ſo , that Dnalgne
flowed in abundance and plentie of all things,
whatſoeuer are neceſſarie foz the vſe and ſu-
ſtentation of man in this life, and other nations (pzouided that they bee our freendes
                                                and

and of chzistian religion) wanted the same,
then would I wishe that some of our superflu-
itie might be erogate to them, to the supplie of
their necessities, but not otherwise . And this
standeth both with the lawes of God, charitie,
and good conscience.

Theod. These are marueilous sleights to
get mony withall. But I pray you haue they
no moze?

Amphil. They want none I warrant you,
foz rather than to faile, they haue their false
waights, their counterfet ballanc s, their a-
dulterate measures, and what not, to deceiue
the poze people withall, and to rake in mony.
But the Wise man telleth them, that false
baliances, counterfet weightes, and vntrue
measures are abhomination to the Lozd. And
the Apostle telleth them, that God is the iust
reuenger of all those that deceiue their bze-
thzen in bargaining. And yet shall you haue
them in the sale of their wares to sweare, to
teare, and protest, that befoze God, befoze Iesus Chzist, as God shall saue my soule, as God
shall iudge me, as the Lozd liueth, as God receiue me, as God helpe me, by God and by the
wozld, by my faith and troth, by Iesus Chzist,
and infinite the like othes, that such a thing
cost them so much, & so much, and it is wozth
this

this much, and that much, when in truth they sweare as false, as the liuing Lord is true, as their owne consciences can beare them witnesse, and I feare me will condemne them at the day of the Lord, if they repent not. For if a thing cost them ten shillings, they will not blush to aske twentie shillings for it. If it cost them twentie shillings, they will not shame to aske forty shillings for it, and so of al others, doubling, tripling, and quadrupling the price thereof without either feare of God, or regard of good conscience.

Theod. What say you of the Drapers, and cloth sellers, liue they in the same order that the other doe?

Amphil. Of Drapers I haue little to say, sauing that I thinke them cater cosins, or cosin germans to merchants. For after they haue bought their cloth, they cause it to be tentered, racked, and so drawne out, as it shall be both broader, and longer than it was when they bought it almost by halfe in halfe, or at lest by a good large sise. Now the cloth being thus stretched forth in euery vaine, how is it possible either to endure, or hold out, but when a shower of raine taketh it, then it falleth and shrinketh in, that it is shame to see it. Then haue they their shops and places where they

sell

sell their cloth commonly very darke and obscure, of purpose to deceiue the buiers. But Caueat emptor (as the old saieng is) Let the buiers take héed. For Technas machinant, & retia tendunt pedibus, as the saieng is : They meane deceit, and lay snares to intrap the féet of the simple. And yet notwithstanding they will be sure to make price of their racked cloth double, and triple more than it cost them . And will not sticke to sweare, and take on (as the other their confraters before) that it cost them so much, and that they doe you no wrong. God giue them grace to haue an eie to their consciences, and to content themselues with reasonable gaines.

Theod.   I thinke there is great fault to bee found in the first makers of the cloth, for the naughtinesse thereof, as well as in the Drapers, is there not ?

Amphil.   No doubt of that. For some put in naughty wool, and cause it to be spun & drawne into a very small thred, and then compounding with the Fuller to thicke it very much, and with the Clothier also to sheare it very lowe, and with some liquide matter, to lay downe the wooll so close, as you can hardly sée any wale, and then selleth it as though it were a very fine cloth indéed. Other some mixe god wooll,

wooll, and naughty wooll togither, and vsing it
as before, they sell it for principall good cloth,
when it is no thing lesse. And then for their
further aduantage, euery vaine, euery ioint,
and euery threed must be so tentered and racked, as I warrant it for euer being good after. Now it being thus tentered at his hands,
and after at the Drapers handes, I pray
you how should this cloth be ought, or endure
long?

Theod. Be there Goldsmithes there any
store also, as in some other countries there be?

Amphil. There are inow, and more than
a good meanie. They are (for the most part)
very rich, and wealthye, or else they turne
the fairest side outwarde as manye doe in
Dnalgne. They haue their shops and stalles
fraught and bedecked with chaines, rings,
golde, siluer, and what not woonderfull richly. They will make you any monster, or
antike whatsoeuer of golde, siluer, or what
you will. They haue store of all kinde of
plate whatsoeuer. But what? Is there no
deceit in all these goodlye shewes? Yes too
many. If you will buy a chaine of golde,
a ring, or any kinde of plate, besides that
you shall paye almost halfe in halfe more
than it is woorth (for they will perswade
you

you the workmanship of it comes to so much,
the fashion to so much, and I cannot tell what)
you shall also perhaps either haue that golde
which is naught, or else at least mirt with o-
ther drossie rubbage, and refuse mettall, which
in comparison is good for nothing. And sometimes or for the most part you shal haue tinne,
lead, and the like mirt with siluer. And againe
in some things some will not sticke to sell you
siluer gilt for gold, and well if no worse too
now and then. But this happeneth very seldome, by reason of good orders, and constitutions made for the punishment of them that
offend in this kind of deceit, and therfore they
seldome dare offend therein, though now and
then they chance to stumble in the darke.

Theod. Haue you good wines in Dnalgne?
Amphil. Indeede there are excellent wines
as any be in the world, yet not made within
the Realme, but comming from beyond seas:
which when the vintners haue once got into
their clouches, and placed in their sellers, I
warrant you they make of one hogshead almost two, or at lest, one and a halfe, by mixing
& blenting one with another, & infusing other
liquor into them. So that it is almost vnpossible, to get a cup of pure wine of it selfe at the
tauerne. But harshe, rough, stipticke, and hard
wine,

wine, neither pleasant to the mouth, nor wholsome to the bodie. And notwithstanding that
they gaine (welneare) one hogshead in another,
yet shall their measures, their gallons, pints,
and quarts be so spare, and their prices so hie,
that it is woonderfull to see. And if a poore simple man go to drinke a pint of wine for the
strengthening of his bodie, and for necessities
sake onely, he shall be sure to haue that wine
brought him, that is too bad, though his monie
(J am sure) is as good as the rich mans. But if
a man of countenance come to drinke for pleasure & nicenesse, he shall haue of the best wine
in the seller, though his mony be no beter than
the poore mans. With infinite the like abuses,
which J omit.

Theod. Haue you any thing to say of Butchers, and those that kill and sel meate to eate?

Amphil. Nothing but this: that they are not
behind in their abuses, fallacies, and deceits.
For whereas they pay a certeine price for a
fat beefe, they are so impudent that they thinke
their market is naught; except they may gaine
halfe in halfe, or the best quarter at the least.
And to the end their meate may be more sale-
able to the eie, the fairer, and the fatter, they
will kill their beasts, and suffer the bloud to
remaine within them still, for this cause that

it may incorporate it selfe in the flesh, and so thereby the flesh may not onely be the weightier (for in some places they buy all by waight) but also may seeme both fresher, fairer, newer, tenderer, and yonger. And which is more commonly they vse to blowe, and puffe it vp with winde, to the end it may seeme bigger, fatter, and fairer to the eie. Or if the meate it selfe be leane, and naught, then will they take the fat of other meate, and pin vpon the same very artificially, and all to delude the eies of the beholders. And though it be neuer so old meate, tough, and stale, yet will they sweare, protest, and take on woonderfully, that it is very new, fresh, and tender. So that no more in them than in others, there is little conscience at all. There be some of them also now and then that will not sticke to sell meate which hath died (perchance) in a ditch, if it be worth the eating (which is most lamentable) and yet wil beare the world in hand that it is excellent meate, that it died kindly, and so soorth. So that hereby infinite diseases are caught, and manie times present death insueth to the eaters thereof.

Theod. Is meate deere or good cheape there for the most part?

Amphil. It is commonly deere, seldome good cheape,

cheape, and the reason is, bicause a sort of insaciable cormorants, greedie grasiers I meane, who hauing raked togither infinite pasture, feed all themselues, and will not sell for anie reasonable gaine, and then must the Butchers needes sell deere, when as they buie deere.

Theod. Why? would you haue no grasiers, then how coulde there bee anie meate fatted?

Amphil. Yes I would haue grasiers. But I would not haue a few rich cobs to get into their clowches almost whole countries, so as the poore can haue no releefe by them. For by this meanes pastures and groundes are not onely excessiuely deere, but also not to be got of any poore men for monie, whereby it commeth to passe, that the poore are impouerished, and the rich onlie benefited. Yea so greatly are the poore hereby inthralled, that they can hardly get a peece of ground to keepe so much as a poore cow or two vpon for the maintenance of themselues, and their poore families. This is a great abuse: for by this meanes rich men eate vp poore men, as beasts eate vp grasse.

Theod. Doe the gentlemen and others, take in commons & inclosures (as your words seeme to implie) for their better feeding?

Ainphil:

Amphil. Yea, almost all indifferently. For whereas before was any commons, heathes, moores, plaines, or free places of feeding for the poore and others, euen all in generall, now you shall haue all seuerall, inclosed, and appropriate to a few greedy gentlemen, who will neuer haue inough, till their mouths be full of clay, and their bodie full of grauell. Commons and moores which were woont to be the onely state of the poore, & whervpon eche might keepe cattle, both neate and sheepe, according to his estate, are now taken from them, wherby manie are constrained either to famish, or else to beg their breade from doore to doore. So that in proces of time if these inclosures be suffered to continue, the state of the whole Realme will mightily decay, a few shall be inriched, & many a thousand poore people both men, women, and children, in citie and country, vtterlie beggered. Oh it was a goodlie matter, when the poore man might turne out a cow, or two, & certeine numbers of sheepe to the commons, and haue them kept well vpon the same, both winter & sommer, freely without costing them ought, whereas now they are inclosed, made seueral, and imploied to the priuate commoditie of a few ambicious gentlemen, so as the poore man cannot keepe so much as a pig or a goose vpon

the

the same.

Theod. It is great pittie that such oppression of the poore should be borne withall or suffered in any of what degræ soeuer.

Amphil. It is so. But what than. You shall
haue some that not for the benefit of grafing,
and fæding onely will take in commons, and
inclosures, but also some that for vainegloríe,
worldly pompe, promotion & foolish pleasure,
will not sticke to pull downe whole townes,
subuert whole parishes, and turning foorth all
a begging, rather then to faile, make them
parkes, chases, warrants and I cannot tell
what of the same. And when they haue thus
done, their bucks, their does, their stags, harts,
hinds, conies, and the like, not onely not fead,
intra gyrum suum, Within their circuit, but
eate vp and deuoure all the poore mens fields,
corne, grasse and all. So that it is hard if any
poore mans corne scape their fangs within a
dozen myles compasse, which is a pitifull and
a lamentable case.

Theod. Would you not haue parkes, and
chases for game?

Amphil. I disalow them not. But I would
not haue them to be made of the poore mens liuings, nor yet to stand to the preiudice of the
whole country adioining. Therefore if they
C.3.   will

will haue parkes and chases. First let them see that they be of their owne proper lande, and then that they be no annoiance to the country about, and then let them haue them in the name of God.

Theod.   Be there any grasiers of sheepe there also.

Amphil.   Two manie, if it pleased God. For nowe euerie meane gentleman if he can pretend (though neuer so little) title to any common, heath, moore, or pasture, he will haue it, quo iure, quaue iniuria, Either by hooke or crooke. And wheras before time there hath bin a whole parish or towne maintained vpon the same, now is there no bodie there dwelling, but a sheepeheard and a dogge lolling vnder a bush. Thus are whole parishes and townes made praies to rich grasiers. Yea, you shall haue some grasiers to keepe fiue hundred, a thousand, fiue thousand, ten thousand, twentie thousand sheepe of his owne at one time, now iudge you what infinite commodities ariseth hereof.   Besides that, when they sell their wooll (as though they gayned not inough otherwise) it is a worlde to see what subtilities, (I will not saie what falsities) they vse in the sale thereof. As first, to intermixt and blenke the good and naughtie wooll togi

togither, to winde it vppe clooselie that it
shall not be seene within. And which is
moze, because they sell all by waight, they
will not sticke to vse sinister meanes to
make it pease well in waight. Some lay it
after it is clipped from the sheepes backe in a
moyst seller, vnderneath the grounde to
the ende that the moysture, humiditie, and
wette of the seller may instill into it, and so
may pease the moze. Otherſome will cast
wette ſalt into it, which in time will liqui-
fie, and cauſe it to be the waightier. With
manie other the like wicked sleights, and le-
gerdimeanes, whereof for that I would rather giue them a taſte in hope of amendment,
then a plaine deſcription for feare of diſplea-
ſing them, at this time I will omit to ſpeake
any moze till further occaſion be offered.

Theod. Is the lande there poſſeſſed in common, oz elſe is their propertie in all things,
and ſo conſequently landlozds?

Amphil. There is not onelie a propertie in lands there, but alſo in all things elſe,
and ſo landlozds inow nioze then be good ones
iwis.

Theod. Doe they let out their lands, their
farmes, and tenements, ſo as the pooze tenants
may liue well vpon them.

Amphil. Oh no. Nothing lesse. But rather
the contrarie is most true. For when a gentleman or other hath a farme, or a lease to let:
first he causeth a survcior to make strict inqui-
rie what may be made of it, and how much it
is worth by yeere, which being found out, and
signified to the owner, he racketh it; straineth
it, and as it were so setteth it on the tenter
hookes, stretching euery vaine, and ioint thereof, as no poore man can liue of it. And yet if he
might haue it freely for this racked rent too, it
were somewhat well. But (out alas, and fie for
shame) that cannot be.. For though he pay neuer so great an annuall rent, yet must he pay
at his entrance a fine, or (as they call it) an income of ten pound, twenty pound, forty pound,
threescore pound, an hundred pound, whereas
in truth the purchase thereof is hardly worth
so much. So that hereby the poore man if hee
haue scraped any little thing togither, is forced to disburse it at the first dash before he enter the doores of his poore farme, wherin, what
through the excessiue fine, and the vnreasonable rent, he is scarse able to buy his dog a lofe,
liuing like a begger, or little better all his life
after. The time hath beene, and not long since,
when men feared God, & loued their brethren,
that one might haue had a house, with pasture
lieng

lieng to it, yea god farmes, leases, and livings
for little or nothing. Or (as some hold) for a
Gods penie as they called it. But howsoeuer
it be, certeine it is, that that farme or lease,
which one might haue had then for ten shillings, is now woorth ten pound. For twentie
shillings, now is woorth twentie or threescore
pound. For fortie shillings, is now woorth
fortie pound, or an hundred pound and more.

Theod. Then I perceiue, they let not out
their land after the old rent: doe they?

Amphil. No. You may be sure of that, they
loue nothing woorse. They cannot at any hand
broke or digest them that would counsel them
to that.

Theod. Why? Haue not landlords authoritie, and may they not make as much of their
owne lands as they can? They count that good
policie, and I haue heard them say, Is it not
lawfull for me to liue vpon mine owne, and
to get as much for it as I can?

Amphil. They must first consider that the
earth is the Lords (as the Psalmograph saith:
Domini est terra, & plenitudo eius. The
earth is the Lords, and the fulnesse thereof)
and all that dwelleth therein. And therefore
being the Lords in propertie, it is theirs but
in vse onely. And yet not so. But that they
ought

ought to lay it foorth to the ſupport of the poore,
that all may liue iointly togither, & maintaine
ÿ ſtate of the common wealth to Gods glorie.
For otherwiſe if a few rich cobs ſhuld haue al,
& the poore none, it ſhuld come to paſſe, that the
ſtate of the common wealth would ſoone decay, &
come to confuſion. They ought alſo to conſider
how they came by their lāds, whether by right
or wrong. If by right, then are they bound by
Gods lawe, and good conſcience to let foorth the
ſame ſo as the poore may well liue vpon them.
But if they poſſeſſe thē wrongfully, then ought
they to ſurrender their tytle, and giue it to the
right heire: but take them with that faull & cut
of their necks. No man ought to poole and pill
his brother, nor yet to exact, and extort of him
more than right, & reaſon requireth, being ſure
that the ſame meaſure which he meaſureth to
others, ſhal be meaſured to him againe. Euery
one muſt ſo deale with his owne, ſo let it out, &
ſo liue as others may liue by him & not himſelf
alone, for the earth is comon to al Adams children, & though fortune haue giuen more abundance to ſome than to other ſome, yet dame nature hath brought fooorth al alike, & wil receiue
them againe into hir wombe alike alſo. And
therefore ought euerie chriſtian to doe to o-
thers, as they would wiſh to be done to, which
lawe

lawe if it were obserued well, would cut of al
oppression whatsoeuer.

Theod. I pray you how came noble men,
and gentlemen by their lands at the first?

Amphil. Cicero saith that in the beginning
before the world was impeopled men comming
into huge & wast places inhabitable, either toke
to théselues asmuch land as they would or else
wan it by ý sword, bought it by purchase, had
it by gift, or else recciued it from their forefa-
thers, by lineal discent, or hereditary possessió.
Which saieng of his must nædes be true both
in the people of the former world & in vs also.
Then seeing this is so, ought not euery good
christian to set forth his lande so as poore men
may liue vpon it aswel as himselfe:whosoeuer
doth not this,eschewing al kind of exaction polling,pilling & shauing of his poore tenants, he
is no perfect member of Christ, nor doth not
as he would be done by.

Theod. You talked before of fines, and incomes,what if a poore man be not able to pay
them, what then?

Amphil. Then may he go sue figmole,for house
gets he none, ý deuil shal haue it before him,if
he will giue him mony inough:no, if ý fine be
not paid (thogh ý rent be neuer so gret) he shall
haue a fig, assone as a house. If ý a poore man
haue got neuer so litle a stock to liue vpon,& to
maintain

maintaine his occupation or trade withall, yet shall he be constrained to sell the same, yea, peraduenture all the goods and implements he hath to pay this fine, so that during the whole terme of his life, he shall hardly recouer the same againe. And then his lease being expired, out of doores goes he, for that he is not able to pay as great a fine or greater than before. Thus are many a one with their wiues, children, and whole families turned out a beging, and die not a fewe of them in extreeme miserie.

Theod. I thought one might haue had a farme, or a lease for a reasonable rent yeerely, without any fine or income paieng.

Amphil. One would thinke so. For paieng as much yeerely, as can be made of the thing it selfe, I wonder what deuill put it into their heads, to receiue such fines and incomes to vndoe the poore withall. The deuill himselfe I thinke will not be so straite laced, nor yet so nigard to his seruants, as they are to their poore tenants. For whereas they will not let out a farme or a lease for one and twentie yeeres without a great fine, the deuill will giue them his whole territorie and kingdome of hell, to their inheritance for euer, and that freely, paieng nothing for the same. And yet notwithstanding

standing all this. There are some landlords,
(nay lewdlords) that hauing racked their
rents to the vttermost, exacted fines, & made
all that euer they can of their farmes, will yet
proceede further, and as men neuer content
with inough, will haue their poore tenants to
pay a yeere or two yeeres rent before hande,
promising them (before they haue it) that they
shall pay no more rent yeerelie, till the same be
runne vp. But when they haue it, they pay
their yeerely rent notwithstanding, and neuer
receiue any restitution for the other. And at
euerie change forsooth they must take newe
leases, and pay new fines, being borne in hand
that their leases before are insufficient, and of
no effect. And sometimes foure or fiue yeres
yea, ten, twentie, fortie, or fiftie yeeres before
their former lease be expired, shall they be constrained to renue their leases, and disburse
great somes, or else haue their houses taken o-
uer their heads. Besides, as though these pol-
lages and pillages were not ill inough, if their
leases be not warely and circumspectly made
(all quirks, and quiddities of the lawe obserued) they will finde such meanes (or else it shal
go verie hard) that the poore man shall for-
fait his lease, before his lease be expired: which
thing if it happen, out goes the poore man,

come

come on it what will.

Theod. Are the instruments, the writings, & conueiaces in that land so intricate, as they are hard to be kept, for so I gather by your words?

Amphil. Yea truly. For whereas in times past when men dealt vprightly, and in the feare of God, sire or seuen lines was sufficient for the assurance of any péce of land whatsoeuer, now 40.60.100.200.500. nay a whole skin of parchment, and sometimes 2.or 3.skins will hardly serue. Wherin shalbe so many promises, so many circumstances, so many exceptions, particles, & clauses, & so many obseruances, that it is hard for a poore ignorant man to kéep halfe of thé: and if he fail in one of the lest, you knowe what followeth. In former time a más bare word was sufficient, now no instrument, band, nor obligation can be sure inough. Fy vpon vs, what shal becom of vs? wa are they of whom the prophet speaketh, saieng : There is no faith, there is no truth nor rightcousnes left vpon the earth. God be mercifull vnto vs.

Theod. Seing that farms, and leases are so deere, I am persuaded that euerie thing else is deere also : is it not so?

Amphil. Yea truly it cannot be chosen. And yet it is strange, that in abundance of althings there shuld be dearth of all things, as there is.

Theod. Who is it long of, can you tell?

Amphil

Amphil. Truly of the landlords onlie in my simple iudgment: for whenas they inhance the rents, & set their fines on tenter as they do, how should the poore man do? Must he not sel al his things a great deale the deerer: Else how shuld he either saue himselfe, pay his rent, or maintaine his familie? so that these greedy landlords are the very causers of al the derth in Dnalgne for truly they are worse than the caterpillers & locusts of Egypt, for they yet left some thing vndeuoured, these nothing, they spoiled but for a time, these for euer: those by commandement from God, these by commission from the diuel.

Theod. How I pray you doe these iollie fellowes spend these wicked gotten goods?

Amphil. I shame to thinke, & I blush to tell you how. For, for the most part, they spend it in dicing, carding, bowling, tennise plaieng, in rioting, feasting, & banketing, in hauking, hunting, & other the like prophane exercises. And not onlie vpon these things do they spend their goods (or rather the goods of the poore) but also in pride their Summū gaudiū, & vpon their dansing minions, that minse it ful gingerlie God wot, tripping like gotes that an egge wold not breck vnder their feet. But herof inough, & more than perchance wil plese their deintye humors.

Theod. Do they exceed in pride of apparel, or are they very teperate, & sober minded people?

Amphil.

Amphil. They are not onely not inferior to any nation in the world in the excesse of apparell, but are farre woorser, if woorser can be, For the taylers doe nothing else but inuent new fashions, disguised shapes, and monstrous formes of apparell euery day. Yea surely I thinke they studie more in one day for the inuention of new toies, and strange deuises in apparell, than they doe in seauen yeeres, yea, in all the daies of their life for the knowledge of Gods word.

Theod. Me thinke then by your reasons it seemeth, that Tailors are the causers of all that monstrous kind of attire worne in Dnalgne, and so consequently are guiltie of all the euill committed by the same.

Amphil. You say very truly. For Mali alitiuius author, ipsius mali, & malorum omnium quæ ex inde orientur, reus erit coram Deo, The author of any euill, is not onely giltie before God of the euill committed, but also of all the euill, which springeth of the same. Therefore I would wish them to beware, & not Cõmunicare alienis peccatis, To be partakers of other mens sinnes, for be sure they shall finde inough of their owne to answer for. But so far are they from making conscience hereof, that they heape vp sinne vpon sinne. For if a man

aske

aske them how much cloth, veluet, oz silke wil
make a cote, a dublet, a cloke, a gowne, hosen,
oz the like, they must néds haue so much, as
they may gaine the best quarter thereof to
themselues. So play they with the lace also: foz
if tenne yards would serue, they must haue
twentie, if twentie would serue, they must
haue foztie, if foztie woulde serue, they must
haue sirtie, if sirtie would serue, they must
an hundred, and so fozward. Besides that, it
must be so dzawne out, stretched, and pulled in
in the sowing, as they get the best quarter of it
that way to. Then must there as much go foz
the making, as halfe the garment is wozth.
Besides this, they are in league, and in sée
with the Dzapers and Clothsellers, that if a
man come to them to desire them to helpe
them to buy a péece of cloth, and to bzing them
where good is, they will straightway conduct
them to their féer, and whatsoeuer pzice hee
setteth of the cloth, they persuade the buier
it is good, and that it is wozth the money,
whereas indéed it is nothing so, noz so. And
thus they betwirt them diuide the spoile, and
he (the tailoz) receiues his wages foz his faithfull seruice done. If a man buy a garment of
them made, hee shall haue it very faire to the
eie (therfoze it is true: Omne quod gliscit non

est

est aurum, (Euerie faire thing is not the best) but either it shalbe lined with filthie baggage, and rotten geare, or else stretched & drawne out vpon the tenter, so as if they once come to wetting, they shrinke almost halfe in halfe, so as it is a shame to sée them. Therefore I aduise euery one to sée to his garments himselfe, and according to the old prouerbe : Sit oculus ipsi coquus, Let his eie be his best cooke, for feare lest he be serued of the same sawce, as manie haue béene to their great hinderance.

Theod. I haue heard it saide that they vse great ruffes in Dnalgne, do they continue them still as they were woont to doe, or not?

Amphil. There is no amendement in any thing that I can sée, neither in one thing nor in other, but euery day woorser and woorser, for they not only continue their great ruffes still, but also vse thé bigger than euer they did. And wheras before they were too bad, now they are past al shame & honestie, yea most abhominable and detestable, and such as the diuell himselfe would be ashamed to weare the like . And if it be true, as I heare say, they haue their starching houses made of purpose, to that vse and end only, the better to trimme and dresse their ruffes to please the diuels eies withall.

Theod. Haue they starching houses of purpose made to starch in? Now truly that passes

of

of all that euer I heard. And do they nothing in those brothell houses (starching houses I should say) but onelie starch bands and ruffes?

Amphil. No, nothing else, for to that end onely were they erected, & therfore now are consecrate to Belzebub and Cerberus archdiuels of great ruffes.

Theod. Haue they not also houses to set their ruffes in, to trim them, and to trick them as well as to starch them in?

Amphil. Yea marry haue they, for either the same starching houses (I had almost said farting houses) do serue the turn, or else they haue their other chambers and secret closets to the same vse, wherein they tricke vp these cartwheeles of the diuels charet of pride, leading the direct way to the dungeon of hell.

Amphil. What tooles and instruments haue they to set their ruffes withall. For I am persuaded they cannot set them artificially inough without some kind of tooles?

Amphil. Very true: and doe you thinke that they want any thing that might set forth their diuelrie to the world? In faith sir no, then the diuell were to blame if he should serue his clients so, that maintaine his kingdome of pride with such diligence as they doe. And therefore I would you wiss it, they haue their tooles and instruments for the purpose.

F. 2.   Theod.

Theod. Whereof be they made I pray you, or howe?

Amhpil. They be made of yron and stéele, and some of brasse, kept as bright as siluer, yea and some of siluer it selfe, and it is well, if in processe of time they grow not to be gold. The fashion whereafter they be made, I cannot resemble to any thing so well as to a squirt, or a squibbe, which little children vsed to squirt out water withall, and when they come to starching, and setting of their ruffes, than must this instrument be heated in the fire, the better to stiffen the ruffe. For you know heate will drie, and stiffen any thing. And if you woylde know the name of this goodly toole, forsooth the deuill hath giuen it to name a puffer, or else a putting sticke, as I heare say. They haue also another instrument called a setting sticke, either of wood or bone, and sometimes of gold and siluer, made forked wise at both ends, and with this (Si diis placet) they set their ruffes. But bicause this cursed fruit is not yet grown to his full perfection of ripenesse, I will therefore at this time say no more of it, vntill I here more.

Theod. What is the leather in that country excellent good, and wel tanned, or but indifferently. I haue heard some complaine of it.

Amphil.

Amphil. There is of both sorts as of all things else, but as there is some naught (I can not denie) so is there othersome as good, as any is vnder the sunne. And yet I must needes confesse, there is great abuse in the tanners, makers, curriers, and dressers of the same: for you shall haue some leather scarcely halfe tanned, so that within two or three daies or a week wearing (especially if it come in any weat) will straight way become browne as a hare backe, and which is more, fleete and run abroad like a dishclout, and which is most of all, will holde out no water, or very little. And the saieng is (*Erubesco dicere,* I shame to speake it) that to the ende they may saue lyme and barke, and make the speedier returne of their mony, they will take vp their hides before they bee halfe tanned, and make sale of them. And as herein they are faultie and much to be blamed, so in the surprising of their hides, they are worthie of reprehension. For that which they buy for ten shillings, they will hardly sell for twentie shillings, that which they buy for twentie shillings they will not willingly sell for fortie shillings . And thus by this meanes, they make shooes vnreasonable deere.

Theod. Then the fault is not in the shoomakers onely, that shooes be so deere ?

Amphil.

Amphil. There is fault inough in them also. For wheras the others inhanse the prize of their hides excessiuely, these felowes, racke it very vnconcionably. And yet if the shwes were good, though dære, it were somwhat tollerable, but when they shall be both naught, and yet dære to, it is to bad, and abhominable. Now if you aske the shoomakers in whom the fault doth consist, they will answere you strait in the tanner. But this is certeine, that as there is a horrible fault in the tanner, so there is more, or as much in the shoomaker. For first of all the shoomaker liquoreth his leather, with waterish liquor, kitthen stuffe, and all kinde of baggage mingled togither. And as though that were not ill inough, they saie they vse to put salt in the liquor, wherewithall they grease the leather of purpose, to the ende that the leather shal neuer hold out water. And truelie it is verie likelie, they doe so, or some such like thing, for surelie almost none of their leather will holde out water, nor scarselie durt neither. Besides this it is a worlde to see how lowsely they shall be sowed, with hotte alles, and burning threedes, euerie stitche an inch or two from another, so as with in two or three daies you shall haue them seamerent and all to betorne. And yet as though this were not
ill

ill inoughe they adde moze. Sometimes they
will ſell you calues leather foz cow leather,
hozſe hides foz oxe hides, and truelie I thinke
rotten ſhæpe ſkins foz good ſubſtantial & dure=
able ſtuffe. And yet ſhall a man pay foz theſe as
well as foz better ſtuffe. And to the ende
they may ſæme gaudie to the eie, they muſt
be ſtiched finelie, pincked, cutte, karued, ra=
ſed, nickt, and I cannot tell what. And good
reaſon, foz elſe would they neuer be ſold. The
inwarde ſole of the ſhoe commonlie ſhall be
no better then a cattes ſkinne, the heeles of
the ſhoes ſhall be little better. And if the
ſooles be naught (as they be indeede, yet
muſt they be vnderlaied with other peeces
of leather, to make them ſeeme thicke, and
excellent ſtuffe, whereas indeede they are
nothing leſſe. And to make the ſooles ſtiffe,
and harde, they muſt be parched befoze the
fire, and then are they moſt excellent ſooles,
And ſuch as will neuer be wozne, no I
thinke not in halfe a coopple of daies, which
is a woonderfull thing. Oh, farewell foz=
mer wozlde, foz I haue hearde my Father
ſaie, and I thinke it moſt certeinely true,
that a paire of ſhooes in thoſe daies woulde
haue kept a man as dzie as a feather, though
he had gone in water all the daye thozowe,

yea,

yea, all the weeke thorow, to the very last day,
and would haue serued a man almost a whole
yeere togither, with a little repairing. But
now fiue or sixe paire, halfe a scoze, yea, twentie paire of shoes will scarsely serue some a
yeere, such excellent stuffe are they made of.
But let all shoemakers tanners, and the rest,
take héed, for at the day of iudgement they shal
render accounts for this their doing. And hereof hitherto.

Theod. Be there any Brokers, or such kind
of fellowes in your country?

Amphil. If it be a thing that is good, it is a
doubt whether it be there, or no, but if it bee
naught (as brokerie is) then past peraduenture
it is there.

Theod. What maner of fellowes are those
Brokers, for truly their profession, and the vse
thereof is vnknowne to me, saue onely that
I haue heard of some of their dealings?

Amphil. Seeing that you are ignorant of
this goodly mysterie, and high profession of
brokerie, and also so desirous to knowe the
truth of them, I will in few words (as briefly
as I can) declare vnto you the substance thereof. These Brokers are iolly fellowes forsooth,
and such as in the beginning of their occupation, haue either iust nothing, or else very little
                                                              at

at all, who when they haue attempted, and aſ-
ſaied by all kind of meanes, and waies to liue,
and cannot by any of them al either any thing
thriue, oz which is leſſe, not ſo much as maintaine their poze eſtate withall, though but
meanly, then fall they into acquaintance with
looſe, diſſolute, and licentious perſons, either
men oz women, to whom all is fiſh that comes
to net, and who haue limed fingers, liuing vpon pilfering, and ſtealing, and of theſe they buy
foz little oz nothing, whatſoeuer they ſhal haue
filched from any. And thus by this meanes in
pzoceſſe of time, they feather their neſts well
inough, and growe (many of them) to great
ſubſtance and wealth.

Theod. Will they buy any thing whatſoeuer commeth to hand?

Amphil. Yea all things indifferently without any exception. All is good fiſh with them
that comes to net. They will refuſe nothing
whatſoeuer it be, noz whom ſoeuer bzingeth
it, though they be neuer ſo ſuſpitious, no although it be as clære as the day, that it hath
bæne purloined by ſiniſter meanes from ſome
one oz other. And can you blame them? Foz
why? They haue it foz halfe it is wozth.

Amphil. What wares be they (foz the moſt
part) which theſe Bzokers doe buy and ſell?

Amphil.

Amphil. I told you they wil refuse nothing.
But especially they buy remnants of silks, veluets, satins, damasks, grograins, taffeties, lace
either of silke, gold, siluer, or any thing else that
is worth ought. Othersome buy cloakes, hosen
dublets, hats, caps, coates, stockings, & the like.
And these goodly marchandize, as they haue
them good cheape, so they will sel them againe
to their no small gaines.

Theod. If this be true, that they will receiue
all, and buy al that comes to hand, than it must
needes be that this is a great prouocation to
many wicked persons, to filch & steale whatsoeuer they can lay their hands vpon, seing they
may haue such good vent for ye same? Is it not?

Amphil. You say very true. And therfore I
am perswaded that this dunghill trade of brokerie newly sprong vp, & coined in the deuils
minting house the shoppe of all mischiefe hath
made many a theefe moe then euer would haue
bin, & hath brought many a one to a shameful
end at Tiburne, & else where. Yea I haue hard
prisoners (and not any almost but they sing the
same song) when they haue gone to execution
declaime, & crie out against brokers. For saie
they, if brokers had not bin, we had not com
to this shamefull death, if they would not haue
receiued our stollen goods, we woulde neue
haue

haue stollen them, and if we had not stollen them we had not bin hanged.

Theod. Then it semeth by your reasons, that brokers are in effect accessary to the goods feloniouslie stolen, & are worthie of ý same punishment ý the others that stale thē are worthy of?

Amphil. They are so, if before they buy them they know precisely that they are stolen, & yet notwithstanding will not onely willingly buy them, but also rather animate, than disanimate them to perseuere in their wickednes, as this their greedy buieng of their wares doth argue ý they doe. This maketh many a tailer to aske more cloth, more silk, veluet, & lace, than he nedeth, & all to the ende the broker may haue his share, for be they neuer so litle scraps or shreds or short ends of lace, or smal peces, of veluet, satan, silk or ý like, the broker wil giue mony for thē, with a wet finger. This maketh many seruāts to pilfer, filch, & purloin frō their masters, some a yard or two of veluet, satin, taffety, lace silk, & what not, some hats cots, cloks, & the like & some one thing, some another: this hindereth the merchant man, is discomodious to ý tailer, & beneficial vnto none, but to thēselues: & therfore as they be the seminaries of wickednes, so I besech God, they may be supplanted, except they amend, which I hardly looke for at their hands.

Theod.

Theod. What woulde you haue them to do, that they may exercise their trade, with good conscience, both before God, and the world?

Amphil. I would wish them to doe thus, which if they would doe, they might vse their trade in the feare of G O D, both with good conscience before the Lord, with honestie before the world, and finallie to the lesse detriment of the common wealth. First let them be sure, that the goods which they buy be truely and iustly come by of the sellers thereof. And to the end, that herein they may not be deceiued. Let them examine the matter strictly, where they had it, whose it is, vpon what occasion they would sel it. And in conclusion not to buy it, vntill they haue gone themselues to the right owners of the goodes, and if they find all things well, that they may with good conscience buy it, let them giue reason for it, else not. And if euery brooker would deale thus, their would not so many false knaues bring them such lauish of stollen goods, as they do, neither should their trade grow as it doth into hatred, and contempt.

Theod. You saide before (except I be deceiued) that if they know before they buy any wares, that the same is stollen, if they than buy them, they are accessary to the same goods so
feloniously

feloniously stollen, & so are woorthie of the same punishment, that the principals are woorthie of, I pray you what punishment is inflicted vpon accessaries in Dnalgne.

Amphil. Accessories are punishable by the lawes of Dnalgne with the same punishment that the principals are to be punished withall (for so the lawe standeth) but in the execution thereof, we see the cleane contrarie practised. For when as a theefe, or a fellon stealeth any thing, hee bringeth it to his receiuer, who though he knowe it to be stolen, yet with alacritie admitteth it into his custodie, and reteineth it, hereby making himselfe accessorie, and guiltie of the felonie committed. And yet notwithstanding when execution is to be done for the same, the principall is (peraduenture) hanged vp, the other that is the accessorie is not once spoken of, nor none can saie blacke is his eie. But howsoeuer it be, I cannot be otherwise persuaded, but that the receiuers, and accessories are a great deale more woorthie of death (by the penall lawes) than he who stealeth the thing it selfe whatsoeuer it be. Bicause if they had not any to receiue their stolen goods they would not steale at all. And therefore are the receiuers (in my simple opinion) rather the authors, and the principals (especially if
they

they know befoze they receiue it, that it is ſto-
len) then they that commit the fact, and being
the authozs of the euill comitted, they are to be
puniſhed rather than the perpetratozs of the
fact it ſelfe. But foz want of due puniſhment
to be erecuted as well vppon the one as vppon
the other, we ſæ grœuous crimes, and flagicious facts without all remozſe, oz feare of God,
daily committed. Good lawes there are, both
foz the reprelling of theſe, and al other enozmi-
ties whatſoeuer, but the want of the due ere-
cution thereof, is the cauſe why all wickednes
and miſchiefe dooth reigne and rage euerie
where as it doth, God amend it if it be his good
pleaſure. And thus much bziefly of the noble
ſcience of bzokerie.

Theod.   What hoſpitalitie is there kept, oz
reliefe foz the pooze?

Amphil.   Uery ſmal. Foz as foz the pooze tenants and comons, they are not able to maintaine any hoſpitalitie, oz to giue any thing to
the pooze, their rents are ſo raiſed, & their fines
ſo inhanſed, and yet notwithſtanding they miniſter (J am perſuaded) moze relæfe to the poze
than the rich & welthie doe: moze pooze are fed
at their doozes than at the rich: moze clothed at
their hands than at the rich, & moze lodged and
harboured in their pooze houſes, than in the
rich.

rich. But yet can I not denie but that the gentlemen, & others kéepe sumptuous houses, lusty ports, and great hospitalitie, but so as the poze hath the lest part therof, oz rather iust nothing at all. If the pooze come to their houses, their gates be shut against them; where they standing frost and snow, haile, wind oz raine whatsoeuer, are forced to tary two houres, 3. 4. yea sometimes halfe a day, and then shal they haue but the refuse, and the very scraps neither. And well if they haue any thing too, in stéed whereof they are sometimes sent to pzison, clapt in irons, manicled, stocked, and what not. This is the almes that most men giue.

Theod. Then it séemeth that the pooze are simplie pzouided foz?

Amphil. They are so indéed, God amend it. And yet I am not so full of foolish pittie that I would haue all kind of beggers indifferently without any exception to be fed and nourished vpon the sweat of other mens bzowes.

Theod. Doe you make a difference of beggers then? Are there two sozts of them?

Amphil. Yea, there are two sozts. One sozt is of stout, strong, lustie, couragious, and baliant beggers, which are able to wozke, and will not. These at no hand are not to be relieued (foz qui non operatur non manducet, saith

ſaith the apoſtle, He that will not woꝛke, let him not eat)but are to be compelled to woꝛke, and not to liue vpon other mens labours. Foꝛ he that relæueth theſe, maintaineth them in their idleneſſe,and taketh awaie the childꝛens bꝛed,and giueth it to dogs. Theſe are as dꝛone bées,that liue vpon the ſpoile of the pooꝛe bées that labour and toile to get their ſitting with the ſweat of their faces. If ſuch fellowes as theſe will not woꝛke, but liue vpon begging, let them be puniſhed and impꝛiſoned till they be content to woꝛke. The other ſoꝛt of beggers are they,that be old,aged,impotent, decrepite, oꝛ lame, ſicke, ſoꝛe, oꝛ diſeaſed, theſe I would wiſh ſhould be looked vnto : and theſe are they that euerie Chꝛiſtian man is bound in conſci-ence to relæue.

Theod.   What oꝛder would you haue ob-ſerued in theſe reſpects?

Amphil. The foꝛmer ſoꝛt of ſturdie valiant beggers,which are able to woꝛke and will not, I would wiſh them to be compelled to woꝛke, oꝛ elſe not to haue any relæſe giuen them. And if they would not woꝛk,to puniſh them, if that will not ſerue, to hang them vp. But herein I would wiſh a pꝛouiſo , that being content to woꝛke,they might haue maiſters pꝛouided them with reaſonable wages,foꝛ many would faine woꝛke

worke, and can get none, and than if they will
not worke, to Tiburne with them. The other
sort of beggers which are either halt, lame, impotent, decrepite, blind, sicke, sore, infirme, and
diseased, or aged and the like, I woulde wish
that they should be maintained euerie one in
his owne parish, at the costs and charges of the
same. And if the parish be not able to maintain
so manie, then that there should be collections
& contributions made in other parishes to supplie their want; and so the former poore people
to be maintained thereupon. For wante of
which godlie order, and constitution, there are
infinite of the foresaid persons that die some in
ditches, some in holes, some in caues, and dens,
some in fields, some in one place, some in another, rather like dogs than christian people.
For notwithstanding that they be neuer so
impotent, blind, lame, sick, old, or aged; yet are
they forced to walke the countries from place
to place to seeke their releefe at euery mans
doore, except they wil sterue or famish at home,
such vnmercifulnes is in Doalgne. Yea, in such
troups doe they flocke, and in such swarmes,
doe they flow, that you can lightlie go no way,
but you shall see numbers of them at euerie
doore, in euerie lane, and in euerie poore caue,
and as though this were not extremity inough

G.I.   they

they driue them from citie to citie, from parish to parish, from towne to towne, from hundred to hundred, from shire to shire, and from country to country like flocks of sheepe. Here they dare not tarrie for this Iustice, nor there for that Iustice, here for this man, nor there for that man, without a licence or a pasport, wheras a man would thinke their old age, their hoare haires, their blindnesse, lamenesse, and other infirmities should bee pasports good inough for them to go abrod withal, if they cannot get releefe at home. But if the former order that euery parish should maintaine their pore were taken, then should they neither need to go abroad, nor otherwise want their daily releefe.

Theod. Are there no hospitals, spittles, lazar houses, almes houses, nor the like, for the releefe of these pore people?

Amphil. Yes there are some such in cities, townes, and some other places, wherin manie pore are releeued, but not the hundred part of those that want. For the supplie wherof would God there might be in euerie parish an almes house erected, that the pore (such as are pore indeed) might be maintained, helped and releeued. For vntill the true pore indeed be better prouided for, let them neuer thinke to please God. Is it not great pity when a man can passe no wase almost neither citie nor country, but shall haue both halt, blind, lame, old aged, sicke, sore & diseased hanging vpon his sleue, and crauing of releefe : Whereas if the former order were established, then should none at al need to go abroad, but al shuld haue sufficient at home. The reformed churches beyond seas, and euen the French, Duch, & Italian churches in Dnalgne are worthie of great commendations herin, & shal rise vp at the day of iudgment to our condemnation except we repent & amend our vnmercifulnesse towards the poore. These good churches folowing the counsel of the almighty who biddeth that there be no begger amongst vs, suffer neuer a one of their countrymen, nor yet any other dweling in their parish to beg or aske almes without his parish, nor yet in his parish neither, but by mutual contribution and collectious maintaine them, & minister to their necessities in all things, Which thing G O D grant the churches of Dnalgne may once begin to practise amongst themselues, that God may be glorified, and the poore members of Chrift Iefus releeued and maintained.

Theod.   Be there husbandmen there, & such others as manure and till the ground, for the further increase of fruits, to the maintenance of the commonwealth :

G. 3.

Amphil.

Amphil. There are of such indeed good store, and as excellent men in that kinde of exercise, as any be vpon the earth. They know exactly I warrant you, the times and seasons of the yeere, when euerie kinde of graine is to be sowed, and what ground is best for euerie kinde of cornes. They are not ignorant also, howe to culture & dresse the same, and if it be barren what kind of dung is best to fatten the same againe. They know the nature, the propertie, & qualitie of euerie soile, and what corne it will bring. They know also when the ground is to be tilled, when not, how long it will bring forth good corne, how long not, when it ought to rest, when not, with all things else incident to the same.

Theod. I thinke they haue good farmes, and tenemēts, that are able to furnish their ground in this sort, for otherwise they were not able to keepe their oxen, their horses, their seruants, and other necessaries, belonging thereto, haue they not so?

Amphil. No truely haue they not. For some haue such fatte farmes, and tenements, as either will bring forth no corne at all (in a manner) or if it doe verie little, and that not without great cost bestowed vpon it. Other some haue houses with no lande belonging to

them

them at all, and yet notwithstanding shall pay
a good round some for the same also ¶ And no
marueile, for landlords, and gentlemen take
all the lands , and lyuelode wherevpon there
poore tenants shoulde liue into their owne
hands, and suffer not the poore husbandmen to
haue so much ground as will finde them corne
for the maintenance of their poore families, nor
which is more, scarcely to keepe one cow, horse
or sheepe vpon, for their continuall relæfe. Or
if they haue any they shall pay tenne times so
much as it is worth, to their vtter vndoing for
euer. But if landlords would consider that the
earth is the Lords, and all that is therein, and
that it is theirs, but onely in title, interest, and
propertie (hauing the souereigntie, or chieftie
thereof) and the poores in vse and possession,
and if they would remember that the poore
ought to liue vpon the earth as well as they,
than would they not vse such tirannie, such ex-
actions, such pooling, and pilling and the like as
they doe without all compassion.

   Theod   There being such store of husbandmen, and the same so expert in their agri-
culture as your words import they be, it must
needes follow , that there is great plentie of
corne, and all kinde of other graine , and the
same verie good cheape, is it not so?

Amphil. There is great store of corne, and all kind of graine, no nation under the sunne like unto it, but as I told you before, thorowe the insatiable greedines of a few couetous cormorants, who for their owne priuate commoditie, transport ouer seas whole mountaines of corne, it is made sometimes very scarse. Otherwise there would be gret store at al times. And wheras you say it is good cheape, it is nothing lesse, as euerie daies successe prooueth true.

Amphil. How can that be, that there being such store of corne, yet should be deare also.

Amphil. I will tell you. It commeth to passe three manner of waies. First, for that landlords racke there rents so extreemely, and aduance their fines so unreasonably, that the poore man is forced to sell euerie thing deere, otherwise he should not be able to pay his land lord his due, whereas if he had his fearme good cheape, he might afforde to sell good cheap. The second cause is (as I haue said) for that the same is carried and conueighed ouer Seas. The third cause is, thorow a sorte of ingratiors, or forestallers, who intercept euerie thing before it come at the market, or else being come to the market, and hauing money

ney

ney at will, buy vp either all, oz the moſt
part, and carieng it into their celles, and
garners at home, keepe it till time of the
yeere that cozne is ſcarſe, and ſo conſequent-
lie deere. And when there is want of it,
then they ſell it deere, and when there is
plentye, then they make it deerer by buy-
ing it vppe in whole heapes as they doe.
Thus you ſée by this meanes, theſe hel-
liſhe ingratours, and forestallers make cozne
and all thinges elſe deere, all times of the
yeere. Nowe iudge you what a hozrible
abuſe is this foz one man to buy vppe all
things, and that not foz anie neede oz want
in himſelfe, but to ſell it againe, deerer
then they bought it, thereby to inriche himſelfe with the impoueriſhing of many a thouſande.

Theod. Is there not puniſhment foz this
hozrible abuſe, foz me thinke great inconue-
niences doe followe it?

Amphil. There be great penalties, and
forfaitures ozdained, as well foz the repreſ-
ſinge of this, as of any other outragious a-
buſe, but they playe with this as with all
other good lawes, they inuente quirckes,
and quiddities, ſhiftes, and put offes ynough

to

to blinde the eies of the magistrates, and to deliuer themselues (trimly trimly) from the
danger and penaltie of the lawe. For they will
say that they buy but for the necessarie proui-
sion of their owne families, and not to sell a-
gaine. And then when they doe sell it againe,
they will beare you in hande it was of their
owne tillage. Or if this way will not serue the
turne, then procure they another man to buy it
with their owne mony vnder his owne name,
and so to sell it againe when hee seeth tyme,
but who hath the commoditie, iudge you.
But if all these waies faile, then buie they it
couertly, and sell it againe as couertly, and
thus they buy and sell their owne soules for
corruptible monie, which in the last day shall
beare witnesse against them , and consume
them : yea as Saint Iames saith : The monie
which they haue vniustlie got with the polling
and pilling of the poore, shall rise vp in iudgement against them, and the rust thereof shall
eate and deuoure their flesh as it were a can-
ker. But let these iollie felowes (as subtil and
as politike as they would seeme to be) take
heed vnto themselues and beware : for though
they can blinde mens eies, and deceiue their
iudgements, yet let them be sure, that they can
not deceiue the iudgement of the Lord, but he
                                        that

that made the eies shall surely sée, and he who knoweth the secrets of all harts, shall one day declare the same to their perpetuall confusion except they repent.

Theod. VVhat be these husbandmen, honest, plaine dealing, and simple persons, and such as in whom, there is no abuse, or else fraudulent, deceitfull, and craftie persons?

Amphil. They are for the most part verie simple and plaine men in outward appearance yea such as if you sawe them, and heard them talke, you would thinke they had no gall, or that there were nothing in them in the world. But if you looke into their dailie exercises, practises, and déeds, you shall find them as craftie and subtill in their kind, as the diuell is in his, if it be possible. For the simplest of them all, if he make a bargaine with another, he wil be sure to make it so as he himselfe may gaine by it. And it is well too, if the other though neuer so wise, circumspect, or prouident, be not vtterly deceiued (or to speake in plainer termes cosoned at their hands) such subtiltie, such policie, and such craftie conueiance they practise vnder the garment of simplicitie. Yea truly it is growne to be almost their profession to deceiue, defraud, and beguile their brethren, insomuch as they count him a wise man, a worldly felowe,

felow, and such a one as will liue in the world
that can not deceiue, and beguile men in bargaining. This is there Columbina simplicitas,
(Nay rather, Vulpina, et serpentina astutia)
which Christ would haue al his childrē to practise in all things all daies of their life. But so
farre from this christian simplicitie are many,
that their whole life (almost) is nothing else,
than a continuall practise of fraud, and deceit,
as for example. You shall haue some that sending corne to the market to be sould, they will
put good corne in the top or mouth of the bag,
to seeme faire to the eie, and in the bottome
of the sacke, very good also (that when it is
powred forth of the same, it may yet seeme ex-
ceeding good still, but in the middest shall be
neuer a good corne, but such as is mustie sprou-
ted, and naught. Whereof can be made neither
good bread nor drinke, for mans bodie. I haue
knowne othersome, that hauing a barren cow,
and being desirous to put hir away haue taken a calfe from another melch cowe, and so
solde the former barren cowe with hir adul-
terate calfe, for a melche cowe, whereas shee
was nothing lesse. With infinite the lyke
sleights, which for breuities sake I omit.

    Theod.   I perceiue then it is good for a
man to be warie that deales with these simple
fooles:

fooles?

Amphil. It were good so indeede, else
he may chaunce to rough himselfe a dawe for
his labour. For I tell you the foxe for all his
crafte may go to schoole to these felowes, to
learne the rudiments of deceit and craft. Such
skilfull Doctors are they herein. If they
sell you a cow, an oxe, a horse or a mare, they
will set the price on him I warrant you, and
with all will profest and take on woonder-
fullie, that hee is but this olde, and that
olde, this yoongue, and that yoongue. And
which is woorst of all, though they knowe
a hundred faultes by them, yet will they
not reueale anye vnto him that buyeth the
same, which is a playne, and a manifest
deceite before the L O R D E, and one daye
shall be answeared for, I dare be their war-
rante.

Theod. Would you haue euerie man to declare to the buyers the faultes and imperfections, which they knowe to be in those thinges
that they sell, then shoulde he sell but a little?

Amphil. Euery true christian ought to do so,
or else besides that he doth not to others, as he
would wish to be done to (for this is the chaine
wherwith euery christiā is bound to another,)
he also breketh the cords of charity & commiteth

most

most horrible cosonage, and wilful presumptuous deceit before God, which is a fault punishable in the iustice of God, with eternall death, in the lake that burneth with fire and brymestone for euer. And seing we ought to doe to others as we would wish to be done vnto vs, let the deceiuer aske of himself when he goeth about to deceiue, these questions. Would I my selfe be deceiued? Would I be cosoned? Would I be vndone and spoiled? Would I count him an honest man, or a good christian that would supplant me in bargaining? Oh no. No more ought I to doe to others, that which I would not should be done to my selfe. Besides this, consider that the apostle saith, The Lord is the reuenger of all such as deceiue their brethren in bargaining. If they would fall into this or the like consideration I doubt not, but fraude, deceit, lieng, dissimulation coosonage, & guile, would be abandoned and put to flight in shorte time which God grant.

Theod. Well, notwithstanding I cannot see how we could liue without husbandmen anie maner of waie, could we?

Amphil. No truly. Neither king, prince, earle, duke, lord, knight, esquire, high nor low, rich nor poore, nor yet any potentate, power or principalitie vpon the earth (how great a monarch

narch soeuer) could liue oz continue without
the vse of husbandzie and husbandmen, And
therefore they are not only to be beloued of vs,
but also to be pzeferred and to be made much
of amongst vs, without whose industrie and
labour no man could liue long vpon the face of
the earth. Foz this cause we read the vse of
husbandzy to be commended vnto vs in sundzy
places of holy scripture, and which is moze the
kingdome of heauen many times to be com-
pared and assimiled to the husbandman, foz diuers purposes and respects. And when Adam
our first parent was expulsed paradise he was
by God himselfe inioined to manure to dzesse
and till the ground, whereby we may see both
the antiquitie, auncientie, and excellencie of
husbandzie, euen from the verie beginning of
all things. And therefoze doubtles is it to be
had in reuerence and estimation of all men.
But hereof inough.

Theod. Be there any Chandlers there as
be in other places?

Amphil. Yea that there are inow I warrant
you, and moze than deale iustly in euerie respect.

Theod. What do they sell foz the most part?

Amphil. Almost all things, as namelie butter, cheese, fagots, pots, pannes, candles, and a
thousand

thousand other trinkets besides.

Theod. What be the abuses which they commit I pray you?

Amphil. Abuses quoth you? They dare not commit anie I trowe. But seeing you would so faine knowe, I will giue you an inkling of them. First they buy that butter, cheese, and other things, which is naught, bicause they may haue it for a little monie, and then sell it for verie good, this manie a poore prentise and other can tell to be true. Or if they buy that which is good, then they either sell it wonderfull deere, or else keepe it till it be past the best, and yet offer it for as much and more than it cost them. Besides this that they keepe their butter & cheese till it be muffie and mould, yea till it smell that no man can eate it, they haue also their false waights & counterfet measures to deceiue the poore people withall. And notwithstanding that they buy sometimes 2. or 3. fagots for a penie, yet wil they not sel one be it neuer so litle, vnder a penie, gaining aboue the one halfe in the other. And as for the stuffe whereof they make their candles, I am ashamed to speake of it. For whereas they should make them of good liquor and sweet, they make them of all kind of kitchen stuffe, & other stinking baggage, so that they shal waste & consume
away

away like vnto ware against the fire, and yet shall neuer burne cleere, nor giue good light, but run ouer, and about the candlesticke too shamefully. And as for the wikes within the, they are of shurds, rope ends, & such other good stuffe. Besides all this they haue sleights to make the liquor of the candles alwaies to remaine soft, to the end it may waste & consume the faster, with legions of the like diuises, God be mercifull vnto vs.

Theod. What say you of the barbers, and trimmers of men, are they so neate, and so fine fellowes as they are said to be?

Amphil. There are no finer fellowes vnder the sunne, nor experter in their noble science of barbing than they be. And therefore in the fulnes of their ouerflowing knowledge (oh ingenious heads, & worthie to be dignified with the diademe of follie and vain curiositie) they haue inuented such strange fashions and monstrous maners of cuttings, trimmings, shauings, and washings, that you would wonder to see. They haue one maner of cut called the French cut, another the Spanish cut, one the Dutch cut, another the Italian, one the newe cut, another the old, one of the brauado fashion, another of the meane fashion. One a gentlemans cut, another the common cut, one

cut of the court, another of the country, with
infinite the like vanities, which J ouerpasse:
They haue also other kinds of cuts innumerable, and therefore when you come to be trimed
they will aske you whether you will be cut to
looke terrible to your enimie, or amiable to
your freend, grime & sterne in countenance, or
pleasant & demure (for they haue diuers kinds
of cuts, for all these purposes or else they lie.)
Then when they haue done al their feats, it is
a world to consider, how their mowchatowes
must be preserued and laid out, from one cheeke
to another, yea, almost from one eare to another, and turned vp like two hornes toward
the forehead. Besides that, when they come to
the cutting of the haire, what snipping & snap
ping of the cycers is there, what tricking, an
triming, what rubbing what scratching, wha
combing and clawing, what trickling & toy
ing, and al to tawe out mony you may be sure
And when they come to washing, oh how gin
gerly they behaue themselues therein.   Fo
then shall your mouth be bossed with the la-
ther, or some that riseth of the balles (for the
haue their swœte balles wherewith all the
vse to washe) your eyes closed must be anoin
ted therewith also. Then snap go the fingers
ful brauely god wot. Thus this tragedy ende
                                              comes

comes me warme clothes to wipe and dry him
withall, next the eares must be picked, and clo=
sed togither againe artificially forsooth. The
haire of the nostrils cut away, and euery thing
done in order comely to behold. The last action
in this tragedie is the paiment of monie. And
least these cunning barbers might séeme vn=
conscionable in asking much for their paines,
they are of such a shamefast modestie, as they
will aske nothing at all, but standing to the
curtesie and liberalitie of the giuer, they will
receiue all that comes how much soeuer it be,
not giuing anie againe I warrant you: for
take a barber with that fault, and strike off his
head. No, no, such fellowes are Raræ aues in
terris, nigrisque similimi cygnis, Rare birds vp=
on the earth, and as geason as blacke swans.
You shall haue also your orient perfumes for
your nose, your fragrant waters for your face,
wherewith you shall bee all to besprinkled:
your musicke againe, and pleasant harmonie
shall sound in your eares, and all to tickle the
same with vaine delight. And in the end your
cloke shall be brushed, and God be with you
Gentleman.

Theod. All these curious conceits in my
iudgement are rather done for to allure and
prouoke the minds of men to be bountifull and
liberall

liberall towards them, than for any good else, which they bring either to the bodie or health of man?

Amphil. True it is that you say, and therefore you must needes thinke they are maisters of their science that can inuent al these knacks to get money withall. But yet I must needs say (these nisities set apart) barbers are verie necessarie, for otherwise men should grow verie ougglisom and deformed, and their haire would in processe of time ouergrowe their faces, rather like monsters, than comlie sober christians. And if it be said that any man may cut off the haire one of another, I answer, they may so, but yet not in such comelie, and decent maner as these barbers exercised therein can doe, and besides they knowe that a decorum in euerie thing is to be obserued. And therfore I cannot but maruell at the beastlinesse of some ruffians (for they are no sober christians) that will haue their haire to growe ouer their faces like monsters, and sauage people, nay rather like mad men than otherwise, hanging downe ouer their shoulders, as womens haire doth: which indeed is an ornament to them, being giuen them as a signe of subiection, but in man, it is a shame and reproch as the Apostle proueth. And thus much of barbers, and their

science.

science.

Theod. Haue you surgeans, and physicians there, as in other places, and are they skilfull and expert in their mysterie, and not onelie skilfull, but also conscionable in their dealings, as well toward the pooꝛe as toward the rich?

Amphil. There are both surgeans and physicians good stoꝛe. And as they be manie, so are they verie vnconscionable in their dooinges, foꝛ as foꝛ both the one and the other so farre from godlinesse and good conscience in all things are they, as if a pooꝛe man that hath not monie to giue them at their pleasure, standes in need of their helpe, they will either not come at him, oꝛ if they doe, they will so handle him, as it were better foꝛ him to be hanged than to sustaine the paines, that they will put him to. But foꝛ the most part, neither of them both will come at him, but rather contemne him, and reiect him as a thing of naught, yea as much will they doe foꝛ the diuell himselfe, as foꝛ a pooꝛe man, if hee haue not money. And againe as long as moneye runneth, they will applye gentle and easie potions, medicines, and salues, bearing their patient in hand that he shall recouer without

all

all doubt, with what disease maladie, oz soze
soeuer he be infected, wheras in truth they can
doe nothing lesse . But Deficiente pecunia,
Monie wanting, they applie bitter potions,
nipping medicines, gnawing cozrosiues, and
pinching plaistures to grǽue their patient
withal, therby to straine out what liquoz of life
(that is what monie oz goods) they are able to
giue. And thus they abuse their gifts to the dis-
honoz of God, the hurt of their felow-bzethzen,
and their owne damnation except they repent.

Theod. Are surgeans and phisitians then
necessarie in a common wealth, as you seeme
to inferre?

Amphil. Salomon saith the Phisition (by
the which wozde he vnderstandeth both the
phisition and the surgean, bicause the one is
coosin germaine to the other) is to be honored
foz necessitie. And if foz necessitie then must
it nǽdes follow, that the same is most necessarie in a common wealth. But as the good, lear-
ued, and discrǽt phisitions and surgeons, are
necessarie, and may doe much good, so the vnlearned, and naughtie (as the wozld is to full of
them) may and doe much hurt dailie as experience teacheth.

Theod. You say truth. But are all indifferently suffered to pzactise the same noble mi-
misteries

ſteries of phiſicke and ſurgerie, without any
choyſe oz exception at all?

Amphil. There is to great libertie permitted herein. Foz now a daies euerie man tagge,
and ragge, of what inſufficiencie ſoeuer, is ſuf-
fered to exerciſe the miſterie of phiſick, and ſurgerie, and to miniſter both the one, and the o-
ther, to the diſeaſed, and infirmed perſons, but
to their woe you may be ſure. Yea, you ſhall
haue ſome that know not a letter of the booke
(ſo farre are they from being learned, oz ſkil ul
in the toongs, as they ought to be, that ſhoulde
practiſe theſe miſteries) both men and women,
yoong and old, that pzeſuming vpon experience
fozſooth (foz that is their greateſt ſkill) will
arrogate great knowledge to themſelues, and
moze then the learnedſt doctoz vpon the earth
will doe. And yet notwithſtanding can doe in
manner nothing at all. But if they chance at
any time to doe any good (as forte luſcus capiat
leporem ſomtime by chance a blind man may
catch a hare) it is by meere chance, and not by
any knowledge of theirs. And yet ſhall this ex-
ploit of theirs be ſounded foozth with a trum-
pet, which indeede may hardly be blowne vp,
with an oten pip- oz any pzaiſe it deſerueth.
This bzingeth the laudable ſciences of phiſick
and ſurgerie, into hatred, obloquy, & contempt,

maketh

maketh it of no estimation in the world, and vtterly discrediteth it amonst men. For when as
any sick, infirmed, or diseased, either miscarieth
vnder the hands of his phisition, or surgean, or
else when the medicine, or salue worketh not
his effect then fall they to accuse the science it
selfe, and to reproch it altogither, whereas in
truth the whole blame consisteth in the ignorance of the practicioner himselfe. Great pitie it
is therefore, that there is such libertie in per-
mitting euery one that lust to prophane and to
abuse, these venerable sciences of phisicke and
surgerie as they doe. For euery man though he
know not the first principles, grounds or rudiments of his science, ẙ lineaments, dimensions,
or compositions of mans body, the poores, arte-
ries, temperament, or constitution, no nor yet
so much as the naturall complexion, qualitie, or
disposition of the same, will yet notwithstanding take vpon him the habite, the title, ẙ name,
and profession of a phisition, or surgean. This
we see verified in a sort of vagarants, who run
stragling (I wil not saie roging) ouer the countries, and beare men in hand of gret knowledg
when as there is nothing lesse in them. By
which kind of theft, (for this coosoning shift is
no better) they rake in great somes of mony,
which when they haue got, they leaue their
cures

cures in the duſt J warrant you, and betake
them to their héeles as to their beſt refuge. And
thus be the noble ſciences of phiſicke, and ſurgerie vtterly reproched, the world deluded, and
manie a good man and woman brought to their
endes, before their time.

Theod. If phiſicke be good, would you not
haue euery man to practiſe it that will, without reſtraint?

Amphil. Phiſicke is good, and yet would J
not haue euerie ignorant doult that knoweth
not the vſe, nor benefit thereof to practiſe the
ſame. For that maketh it to take ſo little effect,
and ſo ſmally to be eſtéemed of as it it is now a
daies (for reformation wherof) J would wiſh
that euery ignorant doult, & eſpecially women
that haue as much knowledg in phiſick or ſur-
gery as hath Jackeanapes, being but ſmatte-
ters in the ſame noble ſciences (nor yet al that)
ſhould be reſtrained from the publike vſe therof, yet not from priuate exerciſe thereof either
for their owne ſinguler benefit, or any other
of their fréends (prouided that they do it gratis)
not making an occupation of it, but rather
for deſire to helpe then for lucre of gaine.
Than woulde J wyſhe that the others who
ſhoulde exerciſe the vſe of Phiſicke and
Surgerie ſhoulde firſt bee Graduates in

either

either of the vniuerſities, and being graduates
yet not to be admitted therefore, but firſt to be
tried and examined as well for their knowledge, diſcreſion, and ſufficiencie in their art,
profeſſion and cailing, as alſo for their godlines, chriſtian zeale, pure religion, compaſſion,
and loue to their brethren, and being found ſuf-
ficient for the foreſaid reſpects, to be admitted
and licenſed, vnder hand and ſeale authentike
by thoſe that be of authoritie. And if he abuſe
himſelfe or his facultie, then out with him, let
him be Officiperda, Iacke out of office, make
him a Quondam, and let him go to plow and
cart, rather than to robbe the poore (as manie
of them doe) yea to murther and kil them without reprehenſion. And as I would wiſh none
but godlie, learned, and ſuch as feare God to be
admitted to the exerciſe and practiſe hereof, ſo
I would wiſh, that either they might be allowed anual ſtipends, for their better ſuccouring
of the poore diſeaſed, or elſe might be conſtrained to take leſſe of their poore patients than
they doe. For now they ruffle it out in ſilckes,
and veluets, with their men attending vpon
them, whereas many a poore man (G O D
wot) ſmarteth for it. Yea, ſo vnreaſonable, and
ſo vnconcionable are they, as ſome of them wil
not ſet one fot out of his owne dores, without
twentie

twentie shillings, fortie shillings, three pound, twentie nobles, ten pound, twentie pound, and some moze some lesse. And hauing this impoztable fée, If they minister any thing to the partie diseased, than besides, must they haue twenty shillings, foz that that stands them not in twentie pins, fortie shillings, twentie nobles, foz that that cost them not twentie pence, & so fozeward. This is a great wickednes, God be mercifull vnto vs, and such as the Lozd will one day reuenge, if they preuent not his iudgements by spédy repentance. Besids these abuses, there are othersome, that if they owe euill will to any, man oz woman being sicke, oz if they hope foz any preferment by their deaths, wil not make any conscience of it, to giue them such medicines, such potions, and dzinkes, as will soone make a hand of them, and this shall be done inuisible in a clowde. Under the pretence of phisicke forsooth, and if he die, why it was not the medicine that killed him (no it were Blasphemia in sanctos ruminare, blasphemie to thinke it of these holie fathers) but it was death that cruell tyger that spareth none. And to such cozruption are they grown that foz mony I am persuaded they can make away with any whom they haue accesse vnto. Therefoze I aduise euery man to be careful to whom
he

he committeth the cure of his booke. They are likewise in league with the apothecaries in whome there are great abuses also, aswell in compounding, and mixing of their elements, & simples togither, as also in selling chalke for cheese, one thing for another, & the like, so as it is hard to get any thing of them that is right pure and good of it selfe, but druggie baggage, and such counterfait stuffe as is starke naught. But of them inough. Let vs speake a worde or two of a certeine kinde of curious people, and vaineglorious, called astronomers, and astrologers, the corruptions and abuses of whom are inexplicable. This done we will make a final ende at this time of speaking any further conserning the abuses, corruptions, and imperfections, of the temporaltie till occasion of more matter hereafter shall be offered.

Theod. These names of astronomers, astrologers, prognosticators, and the like are so vnquoth and strange to my eares, that I knowe not what to make of them. Wherefore I pray you shewe me as nere as you can the meaning of them and what kinde of marchants the professors thereof be?

Amphil The astronomers, astrologers, prognosticators (and all others of the same societie, and brotherhoode, by what name or title soeuer

uer they be called) are a certeine kinde of curi=
ous phantasticall and vaineglorious fellowes,
who secreta dei temere remantes, Searching
the secrets of God rashlie, which he would haue
kept close from vs, and onely knowne to him=
selfe, take vpon them & that vpon these grounds
(forsooth) namely the obseruations of times &
seasons, the aspects and coniunctions of the
signes and planets, with their occurrents, to
presage, to diuine, and prognosticate what shall
come or happen afterwards, as though they sate
in Gods lap, knew his secrets, & had the world
and the disposement therof in their own hands.
It is an olde saieng, and verie true. Quæ supra
nos, nihil ad nos, Those things that are aboue
our reach, conserne vs not, and therefore we
ought not to enter into the bowels & secrets of
the Lord (for as the wise man saith Qui scruta-
tur abscondita dei, obruetur gloria eius, hee
that searcheth out the hidden things of GOD,
shall bee ouerwhelmed with the glorye of the
same, but to content our selues with so much
as hee hath reuealed vnto vs in his sacred
worde, committing the euent, the successe,
and disposement of all thinges else to his
sacrede Maiestie, the GOD of all glorie.
For to them that goe about, and labour
so buselye by speculations, by astronomie,
astrologie,

aſtrologie, and the like curious arts to iudge of things to come, and thinke they can tell all things by the ſame (but Dum parturiunt montes naſcetur ridiculus mus, whilſt the moũtains doe frauell a ſœly mouſe will be bꝛought foꝛth) Chꝛiſt our ſauiour ſaith, Non eſt veſtrum noſſe tempora, & momenta temporum, quæ ipſe pater in ſua ipſius conſtituit poteſtate, It is not foꝛ you to knowe the times and ſeaſons, which the Loꝛd God hath reſerued to himſelfe. And how much our ſauiour Chꝛiſt diſliketh this baine curioſitie, of aſtronomicall, & aſtrologicall ſpeculattons, we may gather by that behement repꝛehenſion, oꝛ commination in the 16. of Matthew, thundꝛed out againſt the people of the Iewes, who were as it ſœmeth tœ much addicted to the ſame. Where he ſharply rebuketh them, and calleth them diſſembling hypocrites, in that they obſerued and marked with ſuch ſerious attention and diligence, the elemental ſignes & tokens in the firmament, being in the meane time, ignoꝛant of greater things, namely of the ſignes and tokens of the ſonne of G O D Chꝛiſt Ieſus, the true Meſſias, and ſauiour of the woꝛld.

Theod.   Uppon what grounds, certeinties, rules, and pꝛinciples doth this curious ſcience conſiſt?

Amphil.

Amphil. It standeth vpon nothing else, but
mæere coniectures, supposals, likelihods, ghes-
ses, probabilities, obseruations of times and
seasons, coniunctions of signes, starres, and
planets, with their aspects and occurrents,
and the like, & not vpon anie certeine ground,
knowledge, or truth, either of the word of God,
or of natural reason. But to argue the vntruth
and the vncerteintie of this foolish curious science, we næd not to go farre for examples and
arguments. For the contrarietie that euer hath
bæne in all ages amongst the verie doctors and
maisters themselues, but most specially of late
doth approue the same to be most fantasticall,
curious, vaine, vncerten, and mære prophane.
For there being a maruellous strange coniun-
ction (as they said) of two superiour planets,
So manie as writ of the same, neither iumped
togither in one truth, nor yet agræd togither
either of the day, houre, or moneth, when it
should be : but in al things shewed themselues
like themselues, that is plaine contradictorie
one to another. Insomuch as they writ in de-
fence of their errors , and confutation of the
contrarie, one against another shamefully to
behold . By which more than presumptuous
audacitie, and rash boldnesse of these, they
brought the world into a wonderfull perplexi-
                                                    tie

tie and ceafe, expecting either a woonderfull alteration of ſtates and kingdomes (as theſe fooliſh ſtarre tooters promiſed) or elſe a finall conſummation, and ouerthrowe of all things. Or if not ſo, yet the ſtrangeſt things ſhould happen, that euer were heard or ſæne ſince the beginning of the world. Wheras God be than-ked at the verie houre, and moment when (as ſome of them ſet downe) theſe woonders and portents ſhould haue happened, there was no alteration nor change of any thing ſæne or heard of, the element being as faire, as bright, as calme, and as pleaſant, and euerie thing as ſilent, and in as perfect order and forme, as euer they were ſince the beginning of the world. By all which appæreth the vanitie, and vncerteintie of their curious ſcience. I woon-der where theſe fellowes ſate, whether vppon the earth, or in the firmament of heauen when they ſawe theſe coniunctions. Or with what eies they could ſæ that, that no man elſe could ſee. But peraduenture they haue Argus eies, and can ſee all things, euen thoſe things that be not. I maruell whether they haue dwelt in the region of the aire, and who told them the names, the ſcituation, the houſes, aſpects, and locall places of the ſignes and planets, of the ſunne, moone, and ſtarres, with the number
                                                                    thereof

thereof also, which indeed are innumerable. I woonder what spirite tolde them which planets were higher than other, and which lower than other, which be good, and which be euill, which be moist, and which bee drie, which bee colde, and which be hote, which be gentle and affable, and which bee cruell and terrible, which giue good fortune, and which giue euill, which be good to take iourneies in hand, or to attempt any great thing, and which bee naught, which bee good for a man to take a wife in, that she may be amiable, and gentle, and which be contrarie, which be dangerous to take diseases in, or to fall sicke, and which bee not, with infinite the like fooleries, which I ouerpasse. Now from whence they haue learned these things I cannot tell, but certeine I am, that out of the booke of GOD, they neuer fetched them, the same being in euerie point contrarie vnto them, and reprouing, yea condemning to hell their vaine curious searching of Gods secrets, and the successe of things by such fallible and vncerteine accidents.

Theod.   Me thinke this is the next way to withdrawe men from GOD the Creator, to depende and hang vpon creatures, is it not?

Amphil.

Amphil. It is the onely waie. For who hearing that the creatures as the sun, the moone, the starres, the signes & planets, doe giue both good things and euil, blessing and cursing, good successe, and euill successe, yea, life and death, at their pleasure (as these brainesick fooles hold they doe) and that they rule, gouerne, and dispose al things whatsoeuer, yea both the bodies & soules of man (for so some shame not to say) who hearing this I say, would not fall from God, and worship the creatures, that giue such blessings vnto man? What can be a néerer way to withdrawe the people not onelie from God, but also to hale them to idolatrie, and wholy to depend vpon creatures as the heathen do to their eternall damnation for euer. But say they, though we giue authoritie, great power, great rule and gouernement to the creatures, yet we giue vnto God the chéefest stroke and the chéefest rule in all things, all other creatures being but the instrumentall, or secundarie causes, or (that I may speake plainlie) as it were his deputies, substitutes, or instrumentes whereby he ruleth and worketh all things. Is this any thing else, than to saie with certeine heretikes, that though God made all things, yet he ruleth them not, nor hath no care ouer them, but hath committed the rule
and

and gouernement of them to his creatures.
Then which what blasphemie can be greater?
is not this a flatte deniall of the prouidence of
God, which scripture so much setteth forth, and
commendeth vnto vs? Shall we thinke that
God made all things, and now as one wearie
of his worke, committeth the gouernmente of
them to other creatures? Saith not our Sauior
Christ Pater et ego operamur, my father worketh, and I worke? Meaning thereby that as he
wrought in creating of all things, so he worketh still in ruling them by his power, gouerne-
ing them by his wisdome, and preseruing them
by hys prouidence, and will do to the end of the
world. But when they haue proued that he hath
committed the rule and gouernement of his
creatures, to his creatures, then I will saye as
they say. In the meane time I say & holde that
it derogateth greatly from the glorie and maiestie of God, to saye or affirme that creatures
haue the gouernement of all things committed
vnto them. For if there should be many kings,
princes and rulers in any one realme or country, must not the dominion and rule of the chief
prince or regent be lesser, than if he ruled, and
gouerned alone? Woe were vs, if wee were
at the rule and gouernement of creatures, but
blessed be our God, who as he knoweth our

I. I.   frailtie

frailtie (hauing therefore côpaßion of our infirmities) so he ruleth and gouerneth all things,
whether in heauen, earth, hell, or else whersoeuer according to the good pleasure of his will.
In the 1. and 2. chapters of Genesis, besides infinit the like places of holie scriptures, we read
that the sun, the moone, the stars, with all creatures else were created & made for the vse and
cômoditie of man, being made subiect to him,
& he constitute lord ouer them. & yet notwithstanding are they becom now his lords, and he
their subiect, vassall, and bondslaue? This is
preposterous geare, when Gods ordinance is
turned topsie turuie, vpside downe. It is time
these phantasticall fellowes were looked to in
time, that wil go about to disthronize the migh
tie God Iehoua of his regall throne of maiestie and glorie, making an Officiperda of him,
a iacke out of office, & to pul him (as it were) E
cælis, Out of the heauens, downe to the earth,
giuing him no power nor authoritie at all.

Theod. Haue the signes and planets then no
power nor authoritie at all vpon things on the
earth?

Amphil. Yes they haue their power, their
operation, force, strength and effect in those
things whereto G O D hath created them, as
namely in the growing, increasing, cherishing,
fostering, renewing, comforting & reuiuing of
all

all natural things, And also they haue their influence & operation in mans bodie, for letting
of bloud, receiuing of purgatiõs, & the like. But
to say that they work these effects of their own
proper force & strength, or that they rule or dispose the spirits & soules of man, is vtterly false
& at no hand true. And yet notwithstanding so
far infatuat are these busie heded astronomers,
& curious serching astrologers, that they attribute euery part of mans body to one particular
signe & planet, affirming that part of the bodie
to be ruled by that signe, or planet. And therefore to Aries they haue assigned the gouernement of the head & face. To Tau. the necke and
throte. To Gem. the shoulders, the armes & the
hands. To Leo the hart and back. To Can. the
brest, stomake, & lungs. To Lib. the raines and
loines. To Uir. the guts & bellie. To Scor. the
priuie parts & bladder. To Sag. the thighes. To
Capr. the knées. To Aqu. the legs. To Pisc. the
féet. And thus haue they & doe beare the world
in hand that the whole bodie of man both In-
terne & externe, within & without, is ruled and
gouerned by the xij. signes, by starres, and planets & not by God only. For the cõfirmation of
which fained vntruth, they pretend the xij. mo-
neths in the yere to be ruled & gouerned by the
xij. signes in the element, and the seuen daies
in the wéeke to be ruled by the seuen planets

also. Besides this they haue their particular houres, times, and seasons, wherein they chiefly worke their effects, and haue greatest strength. So that by their reasons, no moneth in the yere, nor day in the weeke, nor no houre in the day nor night, but it is ruled and gouerned by the influence and constellation of the starres and planets, and nothing is effected or brought to passe, but what they will, and intend.

Theod. Are the signes and planets liuing creatures and reasonable, or insensible creatures, and things without life?

Amphil. They are no liuing or reasonable creatures, it is without all controuersie, but meerely insensible, and without life. And being without life and reason, how is it possible that they should bring life or death (as these felowes hold) sicknesse or health, prosperitie or aduersitie, heate or cold, faire weather or foule, beautie or deformitie, long life or short, or any thing else? And if they be not able to giue these things, how much lesse able are they then to gouerne, rule, and dispose all thinge in heauen, earth, the aire, or else whersoeuer, to ouerthrowe monarchies, kingdoms, nations, countries, and people, and finally to work althings after their owne desire and will? Will they

haue

haue dumbe and vnreasonable creatures to rule the reasonable ? If that were true, why should God be praised either for his mercie, or feared for his iustice and iudgement, and not rather the planets, signes, and starres; which worke all in all in all creatures ? If blessing come by the influence of starres and planets, then let men praise them and not God for the same. And if curses proceed from the starres, let them be feared for them. Briefly if life and death, and all things else come by the force of the elementall creatures, and celestiall bodies, then let them be honoured with divine worship. If these effects issued from creatures, then why should the homicide, the murtherer, adulterer, or wicked person be punished, whereas he might say, it was not I, it was Planetarum iniuria, The force of the planets that compelled me to sinne ? Or why should the godlie man be praised for dooing well, whereas he is inforced thereto, by the starres and planets? In Summa, why should not planets and starres be adored and worshipped as gods, if they coulde worke these effects ? They that attribute thus much to the starres, not onelie rob the maiestie of God of his honour, but also strengthen the hands of the heathen, pagans, infidels, and idolatrous people, to perseuere in their cursed ido-

latrie

latie ſtill. Nay do they not rather ſhake hands with them, that as they woꝛſhip the ſunne, the moone, the ſtarres, fire, water, and other creatures, foꝛ their God, ſo doe theſe woꝛſhip the ſame, though not foꝛ their chiefe Gods, yet foꝛ their ſecond gods, whereby they commit moſt filthie idolatrie and are giltie of moſt hainous tranſgreſſion. Indeede I confeſſe they haue effects and operations, but yet are they not the efficent cauſes of any thing either good oꝛ bad. Otherwiſe than thus, that it pleaſeth the maieſtie of God to woꝛke by them, as by his inſtruments whatſoeuer is his good wyll and pleaſure, and not after any other ſoꝛt.

Theoe. I haue heard of ſome of theſe aſtronomers that would take vpon them to tell a mans foꝛtune, onely by their conſtellation foꝛſooth is it poſſible ſuppoſe you?

Amphil. No at no hand. Foꝛ if it were ſo, that all things were and man himſelfe gouerned, and ruled by the ſtars alone (as who is ſo foꝛſaken of God to beleeue it?) And that they knew the minds, the purpoſes, the intents, the inclination, the diſpoſition & qualities of euery ſtarre, then might it be (peraduenture) true, that they might tell the foꝛtune, and deſteny of any man. But otherwiſe they can tel as much as a hoꝛſe, I would faine learne of theſe ſtarre

gaiſers

gaisers, who teach that man is drawne to good
or euill by the constellations, and influence of
stars, whether all the people that were euer
borne since the beginning of the world, or shal
be borne to the ende of the same, were al borne
vnder one planet or star: For they had all one
fortune, all sinned in Adam, & all were in the
iustice of God condemned to euerlasting fire.
I would know also whether all the Sodomits
and Gomorreans being consumed with fire, &
brimstone from heauen were borne all vnder
one starre or planet: For they had all one destinie, and all one end. Whether all the whole
world in the daies of Noah, was borne vnder
one, and the same star, or planet, for they had
all one destenie, being ouerwhelmed with an
vniuersall deluge. Whether the whole host of
Core, Dathan, and Abiram, were borne all vnder one star, or planet, who had al one iudgmēt
one destinie, and one kind of death. Whether
all the host of Pharao were borne vnder one,
and the same starre, and planet, who all sustai-
ned one kinde of death, and had all one destinie. Whether Esau, and Iacob were not borne
both in a moment, and both at one birth, and
yet had they contrarie natures, qualities, dis-
positions and ends. Finally I would learne of
them, whither none that euer liued since the

first

first beginninning of the worlde, no2 any that shall be bo2ne to the end of the same, hath not, o2 may not be bo2ne in the same houre, and vnder the same planet, & constellation, that Ch2ist Iesus was bo2ne in. If they say there haue not beene any bo2ne in the same houre that Ch2ist Iesus was bo2ne in, common reason, and daily experience would disp2oue them, fo2 there is not one minute of an houre wherein there are not infinite child2en bo2ne into the world. And if they say that there are that haue beene bo2ne in the same houre, and vnder the same starre, and planet, than must it needes follow (if man should necessarily be ruled, gouerned, disposed & affected, acco2ding to the naturall dispositi-on, and inclination of the planets & stars) that he that hath bin is o2 shall be, bo2ne in the same howre, and vnder the same planet o2 star that Ch2ist Iesus was bo2ne vnder, should bee as good & as perfect in euery respect, as Ch2ist Ie-sus himselfe, and so should we haue had manie ch2ists befo2e this time. But God blesse all his child2en from once thinking of any such impie-tie, and blasphemie. By all which reasons and arguments it apeareth manifestly that man is nothing lesse, than ruled, gouerned, o2 destined, after the inclinatio, o2 influence of stars o2 pla-nets, but onely by the liuing God, who doeth

what

whatsoeuer pleaseth him in heauen & in earth. This being so, twise vnhappy be those parents that thinke any moneth, day or houre infortunate for their children to be borne in, or that some be more fortunate and happie than othersome. And thrise cursed be those wicked deuils, that taught them those lessons. What? Doe they thinke that the Lorde is a sleepe those houres, or being wake hath no power to rule? Hath he not made all things pure and good? Then cannot the good creatures of God make vs euil, or incline vs to sinne. But it is the malice of the deuill, the corruption of our nature, and the wickednes of our owne harts, that draweth vs to euill, and so to shamefull destinies, and infamous ends, and not the starres, or planets. Whereof if we were truely perswaded, we wold leaue of when we come to any shamfull end, to saie: Oh, I was borne to it, it was my destonie, and I cannot tell what: whereas in truth we were borne to no such ends. But rather to glorifie our heauenly father by integritie of life & godlines of conuersation, whilst we liue vpon the face of the earth. Certein it is that God by his prouidence, & prescience, doth foresee that such a man through his wickednes shall come to such an ende, yet did not the Lord foreordeine, or foreappoint him to the same, but

but rather dehorteth him from comitting that
wickednes, which may purchase such an end.
Wherefore to conclude. Seing it is sinne that
bringeth man and woman to shamefull ends,
and neither fate, destonie, birthstar, signe, or
planet, constellation, nor any thing else whatsoeuer, let euerie one endeuour himselfe to
serue his G O D truelie, in singlenesse, and
purenesse of heart, and himselfe to liue well
and vprightlie. Walking in the lawes, and
commandements of the Lord, and I warrant
him for euer comming to anie euill end or destinie. That God whom he hath serued, will
keepe him as he kept Sidrach, Misaac, and A-
bednago, from the rage of the fire, Susanna frō
the stake, Daniel, from ỹ chawes of the grædie
lions, & manie others that serued him in feare.

Theod. I haue head some that woulde take
vpon them to tell a man whither he shoulde be
poore or rich, a seruant, or a lord, a theefe or a
true man, cruell or gentle, and what kinde of
trades he should haue prosperous successe in,
how should they doe this?

Amphil. I will tell you how they pretende
to doe it. There are (as they says) certeine
signes in the element (but yet I maruell what
Apollo tolde them so, when they were there,
and sawe them, or how they knew the shape,

and

and proportion of them) as Aries, Taurus,
Gemini, Cancer, Leo, Uirgo, Libra, Scorpio,
Sagittarius, Capricornus, and Piſces, with
their planets, and aſpects, as Sol, Luna, Mars
Mercurie, Jupiter, Uenus, and Saturne. Now
ſay they, he that is borne vnder Aries, (which
is a ſigne in the Nuſquam region, Like to a
ramme, or ſheepe vpon earth) ſhall be a riche=
man and too too wealthie. And whie ſo? Marke
their drownen reaſon. Forſooth becauſe the
rame is a fruitfull beaſt vpon earth, and yeld=
eth to his maſter two or three fleeces a yeere.
Againe he that is borne vnder Taurus (wl ich
is a ſigne (ſay theſe liers) in the element like
vnto a bull, vpon earth) now ſir he that is borne
vnder him, ſhall be pore, & a bondſlaue all his
daies. And why ſo? Mary ſay they bicauſe the
bull on earth is a beaſt vſed to the yoke, and to
much ſlauerie & drudgery. He that is borne vn=
der Leo, (which is a ſigne quoth theſe inglers
like to a lion) ſhal be ſtrong, couragious & fea=
red, of al men, & ſhalbe lord & ruler ouer many.
And why ſo? Bicauſe the lion is a ſtrong & migh=
tie beaſt, & is lord & king ouer all other beaſts.
He that is borne vnder Scorpio, ſhalbe a mur=
therer, a robber, a theefe, and a wicked per=
ſon. Why ſo? Forſooth bicauſe the Scorpien,
is a ſerpent full of poyſon, & malice vpon earth.

He that is borne vnder Gemini shall be rich, and haue manie children, bicause Gemini is a signe of two twinnes. He that is borne vnder Virgo shall be beloued of women, shall be amiable, faire, gentle, and I cannot tell what, bicause maids are so affected. He that is borne vnder Cancer, shall be crabbed and angrie, bicause the crab fish is so inclined. Yee that is borne vnder Libra, shall be fortunate in merchandize, in waights and measures, bicause Libra is a signe of a paire of ballance. He that is borne vnder Sagittarius, shal be a good shooter, bicause Sagittarius is a signe like to a shooter. He that is borne vnder Capricornus shall be a slouenly, ill fauoured, and vncleane fellowe, bicause the gote is a beast filthie, stinking, and vncleane. He that is borne vnder Aquarius and Pisces shall be fortunate by water, bicause watermen haunt the waters, and fishes swim in the same. These be cupstantiall reasons, and well seasoned arguments, and as strong to proue their purpose, as a castell of paper to resist the enimie. Thus you may see they haue no other reasons, than to heape one lie vpon another. As first that these signes and planets in the heauens are like to earthly creatures, then that their natures, and qualities are knowne by the natures and qualities of

earthly

earthly creatures. Iesu God what cunning fel-lowes are these; that can knowe the nature of heauenly bodies, and celestiall creatures, by these terrestriall bodies, and earthly crea-tures? These are profound fellowes indéed, and by all likelihod, haue dwelt long in the clouds that are so perfect in euery thing there, and can iudge of future accidents with such singular dexteritie. By this time I thinke they are ashamed of their profession, therefore I néed to say no more of them, till further oc-casion be offered, beséching the Lorde God to giue them grace to search for the truth of the worde of God, letting all such curious sear-chings of Gods secrets alone to God, who only knoweth all secrets whatsoeuer.

Theod. If you condemne astronomie, and astrologie altogither, as you séeme to doe, then it followeth that you condemne prognostica-tors, and such as make almanacks for euerie yéere, doe you so?

Amphil. I neither condemne astronomie nor astrologie, nor yet the makers of prognosti-cations, or almanacks for the yéere. But I condemne the abuse in them both, and wish they were reduced to the same perfection that they ought, and to be vsed to the same endes and purposes which they were ordeined for.

The

The sunne, the mœne, the starres, and the celestiall bodies whatsoeuer, created by the Lord
not onelie to fructifie and increase the earth by
their influence, but also to shine and giue light
to man in this life, and to diuide the light from
darknesse, the day from the night, winter from
sommer, and to distinguish one season and time
from another . Now how much may make or
conduce to the knowledge hereof, so much I
doubt not is verie tollerable, and may be vsed.
But when we go about to enter into Gods secrets, and to diuine of things to come, by coniectures, and gesses, then make we the same
wicked, and vnlawfull. Therefore prognostic-
cators are herein much to be blamed, for that
they take vpon them to foreshew what things
shall be plentie, and what scarse, what deere,
what good cheape. When shalbe faire weather,
when foule, and the like, whereas indœd the
knowledge of these things are hid in the secrets of G O D, and are beyond their reach,
therefore ought they not to meddle with them
But if they would kœpe them within their cô-
passe, as namely to shew the times and seasons
of the yere, festiuals, vigils, to distinguish winter from sommer, spring from haruest, the
change of the mœoue, the fall of euerie day, the
eclipses, epacts, dominical letter, golden number,

ber, circle of the sunne, leape yéere, and other the like necessarie points, then were their profession laudable, and greatly for the commoditie of the commonwealth. And thus much with their patience be it spoken briefly hereof.

Here ende the abuses of the
Temporaltie.

THE CORRVPTIONS
AND ABVSES OF THE
SPIRITVALTIE

Theodorus.

Auing now spoken sufficiently of the corruptions and abuses of the temporaltie, if I might be so bold, I would request you somewhat to say concerning the corruptions and abuses of the spiritualtie, or (as some call it) of the ecclesiasticall hierarchie. For I am fully persuaded that the one being so corrupt, the other can hardly bee without blemish.

Amphil.

Amphil. I am verie loth to enter into that fielde, the view whereof offereth such store of matter to intreat of, as if I shoulde enter the same, I shoulde rather not knowe where to end, then where to begin. Besides, you knowe the olde prouerbe, Non bonum est ludere cum sanctis, It is not good to medole with these holie ones, for feare of thunderbolts, to insue. But for that he is not onely a false prophet, and a traitor to the truth, that teacheth false doctrine, but as well he that knoweth the truth, and either for feare of death, or desire of life, wil not expresse the same to the world. And for that, not onely the author of any euill or mischiefe is giltie of offence before God. But also he that might by discouerie therof preuent the same, and yet either will not, or for feare of death dares not. And for that as the olde prouerbe saith Qui tacet consentire videtur, he that concealeth the truth, seemeth to consent to errors, for these and the like causes, I will laye downe vnto you some such corruptions and abuses, as seeme to be inormous, and stande in neede of reformation, omitting in the meane time to speake perticularly of all (for that they be innumerable) vntill I see how these fewe will be brouked of them. For it is a point of good physicke you knowe, to see how the former

meate

meate receiued into the stomacke, will be digested, and concocted, before we receiue any more into the same.

Theod. You say very well. Giue me leaue then (by your patience) to aske you such questions, as I thinke conuenient for my further instruction; that by your good means I knowing the truth, may praise God in you, and also haue iust occasion to giue you thanks for the same.

Theod. Aske what you thinke good in Gods name, and I will doe the best that I can, to resolue you in any thing that you shall demand.

Theod. Then this shal be my first demand. Be the churches, congregations, & assemblies there distincted into particulars, as into parishes and precincts, one exempt from another, or are they dispersed here and there abroad, without any order, exemption, or limitation of place at all?

Amphil. Euerie particular church, congregation, assemblie, or conuenticle is diuided one from another, and distincted into parishes, and precincts; which seuerall precincts and parishes are so circumgired and limited about with bounds and marks, as euerie one is knowne of what parish he is, and vnder whose charge he liueth. So that euerie shepheard knoweth his flocke, euerie paſtoz his ſhæpe. And againe euerie flocke knoweth his ſhepheard, and euerie ſhæpe his paſtoz verie ozderlie, and well in my ſimple iudgement.

Theod. Doe you allow then of this partition of churches, and of one particular congregation from another?

Amphil. Yea trulie. It is not amiſſe, but a verie good ozder, foz thereby euerie paſtoz doth knowe his owne flocke, euery ſhepheard his owne ſhæpe, which without this diuiſion coulk not be. Beſides that we read that euen in the apoſtles daies (who wzit to particular churches themſelues, as to the Rom. Cozint. Theſ Phil, &c.) in the daies of Chziſt, & in the times of the pzophets befoze Chziſt, churches, aſſemblies, and congregations were euer diſtincte one from another, & diuided into ſeueral flocke companies, and charges. So that although they had not the name of this wozd pariſh amongſt them, yet had the thing ment thereby in effea

Theod. Then it followeth by your reaſon that there are infinite churches in Dnalgne and I haue learned out of the bok of God, that there is but one true church, and faithful ſpouſ of Chziſt vpon the earth. How reconcile yo theſe two places?

Amphil. Verie well. Foz although there infinit

infinite particular churches, congregations and assemblies in the world, yet doe they all make but one true church of God, which being diuided in time and place, is notwithstanding one church before God, being members of the mysticall body of Christ Iesus, & felow members one of another, so as they can neuer be diuided neither from themselues, nor from their head Christ.

Theod.   Who doe you constitute the head of the vniuersall church of Christ vppon earth, Christ Iesus, the pope, or the prince?

Amphil.   Christ Iesus, whose the bodie is, must needs be, & is the onely true head of the vniuersall church. Then next vnder him euerie christian prince in his kingdom. And as for the pope he is head ouer the malignant church, the church of the diuel, and not of Christ Iesus. No he is so far from being head ouer the vniuersal church of Christ, that he is no true member of the same, but rather the childe of perdition, the first borne of satan, a diuell incarnate, and that man of sin (euen Antichrist himselfe) that must be destroied with the breath of Gods mouth.

Theod.   By whom be these particular churches and congregations gouerned and ruled?

Amphil.   By bishops, pastors, and other inferiour officers.

Theod.   Do you shut out the prince then from gouerning the church?   *Amphil.*

Amphil.   No God forbid. For take awaye Brachium seculare, The lawfull power, and gouernement of the temporal magistrate from the regiment of the church, and ouerthrow the church altogither. And yet notwithstanding the necessitie hereof, the doting anabaptists and brainesicke papists haue most deuilishly denied the same. The anabaptists denie (most absurdly) the authoritie of the magistrate altogither. The papists seing themselues conuinced by the manifest worde of GOD denye not their authority absolutely, but that their authority extendeth to the gouernement of the church, forsooth they vtterly denie, hereby exempting themselues, and plucking away their neckes from vnder the yooke of christian obedience due vnto migistrates, contrarie to the expresse word of our sauiour Christ, and his apostles who saith Omnis anima subdita sit potestatibus supereminentibus ? Let euery soule be subiect to the higher powers, for there is no power but of God. And therefore they are to be obeyed as the ministers of God of all whatsoeuer.

Theod.   Well than I gather thus much that euery king prince, or potentate is supreame head next vnder God, ouer the church of GOD dispersed through his kingdomes, and dominions,

ons, is not this true?

Amphil. Uerie true. And therefore that anti-christ of Rome, hath plaide the traitor a long while, both to Christ Jesus and all christian kings, in arrogating and usurping to be supreame head ouer all the world. Whereas indæd he being a greasie priest, & smered prelate, hath no more authority than other oiled shauelings haue, nor so much neither, and yet that authoritie is but ouer the maligant church of antichrist, and not of Christ Jesus. I beseech the Lord therefore to breake of that power, to grind in peces that stumbling blocke of offence and to wipe off the heads of that monstrous hidra, so as neuer any mo may growe thereof againe.

Theod. Seeing you say that euerie prince is supreame head ouer the church of God within his dominions, what authoritie therfore assign you to the prince to execute in the church.

Amphil. It is the office and dutie of a prince not only to see elected, sent forth, & called, good, able, & sufficient pastours, for the instruction of the church, but also to see that good orders, constitutions & rites be established, and duely performed, that the worde be preached, the sacraments truely ministred, excommunication, discipline and ecclesiasticall censures orderly

K. 3.   executed

executed to the honor of God , and benefit of
his church. But if it be said that these thinges
are to bee executed of the ecclesiasticall persons onely, I answere true it is, but if the ecclesiasticall magistrate be negligent, secure,
slouthfull, and carelesse about the execution
hereof (as who seeth not some be) than ought
the prince to shew his authoritie in command-
ing and inioining them to doe their office. Besides this, it is the office of the prince to see all
kind of sinne, as well in the church men themselues, as in all others of the church seuerely
punished. And though I grant the prince to
haue the soueraigntie and primacie ouer the
church of G O D, within his dominions, yet
my meaning is not , that it is lawfull for the
prince to preach the word , to minister the sacramentes, or to execute the sentence of excommunication, and other ecclesiasticall discipline and censures of the church, but (as before)to see them done of them, to whom it apperteineth. For saith the apostle nemo sumat
sibi, honorem nisi qui legittime , vocatus fue-
rit vt fuit Aaron. And againe, vnusquisque
in ea vocatione, qua vocatus est maneat a-
pud deum? But in times past the papists bare
the worlde in hande, that no temporall power whatsoeuer coulde nor ought not to
meddle

meddle wyth the clergie, and therefore made
they vassals of most christian Princes. Yea
that pernicious antichrist of Rome, in those
daies of ignorance hath not bæne ashamed to
make kings, Queenes, Emperours, Dukes,
Lords, and all other how honorable or noble
soeuer, his lackeis, his pages, his horsekee-
pers, and compelled them to hold his stirups,
to leade his horse, and to prostrate themselues
before him, whilest he trod vpon their neckes.
But God be praised, this great antichrist is
discouered to all the world, and his shame so
laid open, as euery childe iustlie laugheth him
to scorne.

Theod. You said before that the churches
there were gouerned by bishops, and pastors,
how by them?

Amphil. The bishops are graue, ancient,
and fatherlie men, of great grauitie, learning,
and iudgement (for the most part) constitu-
ted by the Prince ouer a whole country, or
prouince, which they call their dioces. These
graue fathers hauing authoritie aboue all o-
ther of the ministerie, in their dioces, do sub-
stitute vnder them in euerie particular church
a minister, or ministers according to the necessitie of the same. And thus doeth euery
bishoppe in hys owne dioces thorow out the
K.4.   whole

whole realme. So that no church how ſmall
ſoeuer, but it hath the truth of Gods word, and
of his ſacraments truly deliuered vnto it.

Theod. Are thoſe preaching prelates that
the biſhops do place in euerie congregation, or
elſe reading miniſters?

Amphil. It were to be wiſhed that all were
preaching prelates, and not reading miniſters
only, if it could be brought to paſſe, but though
all be not preachers, yet the moſt part be, God
be praiſed therefore.

Theod. Be any readers onlie, and not preachers, that is a great abuſe. For I am perſuaded that he that cannot preach, ought not to
ſupplie a place in the church of God to read onlie, how ſay you?

Amphil. It is no good reaſon to ſay bicauſe
all ought to be preachers, that therefore readers are not neceſſarie. But indeed I am of
this iudgement with you, that whoſo can but
read onelie, and neither is able to interpret,
preach, expound, nor explane the ſcriptures,
nor yet to refell and conuince the aduerſarie,
nor to deliuer the true ſenſe and meaning of
the ſcriptures, ought not to occupie a place in
the church of God, as the paſtor thereof. For
God commandeth that the paſtors be learned,
ſaieng: Labia ſacerdotum cuſtodiant verita-
tem,

tem, & ediscant populi verbum dei ex ore eorum, Let the lips of the priests preserue knowledge, and let the people learne the truth out of
their mouthes. And therefore those that haue
not this dexteritie in handling the worde of
God, they are not sent of God, neither are they
Christs vicegerents or pastors to instruct his
flocke. To such the Lord saith: They rule, but
not by me, they run, but I sent them not, they
crie thus saith the Lord, whereas hee neuer
spake it. These are those woll shepheards, and
dumbe dogs, of whom speaketh the prophet,
that are not able to barke against sinne. And
therefore I beseech the Lord to remoue them,
and place able and sufficient pastors ouer his
church, that G O D may be glorified, and the
church edified in the truth.

Theod. Bare reading I must needs say is
bare feeding, but what then? Better it is to
haue bare feeding than none at all.

Amphil. True true. And therefore are not
they more scrupulous than they ought, more
curious than needes, and more precise than
wise, that bicause they cannot haue preaching
in euerie church, doe therefore contemne reading, as not necessarie? This is as though a
man should despise meane fare, bicause he cannot come by better, whereas I thinke it is
better

better to haue meane fare then none at all, or
as though a man bicause he cannot come by the
carnell at the first, will therefore caſt awaie
both the nut and the carnell. It were good (as
ſaith the apoſtle) that all could prophesie, that
is, that all could preach, and expound the truth,
but bicause that al haue not the gift, is therfore
reading naught? And therefore a ſort of noua-
tians lately ſprong vp, haue greatly faulted
herein, in that they hold that no reading miniſters only ought to be permitted in the church
of God, as though (as I ſay) because a man can
not haue daintie fare, therefore it is good to
haue none at all. But to be plaine, as I will
not defende a dumbe reading miniſterie only,
ſo I will not condemne it for neceſſities ſake,
when otherwiſe euery place cannot be ſuffici-
ently furniſhed at the first with good and ſuffi-
cient men as it ought.

Theod.   But it is thought that there are
inow able men in the vniuerſities, and elſe-
where to furniſh euery particular church with
a preaching miniſter?

Amphil.   Truely I thinke there are ſo, if
they were ſought for & preferred: but alas thoſe
that are learned indeed they are not ſought for
nor promoted, but the vnlearned for the moſt
part, ſomtimes by frendſhip, ſomtime by mony

(for

(for they pay wel for their orders, I heare say)
and somtimes by gifts, (I dare not say bribes)
are intruded. This maketh manie a good schol-
ler to languish, and discourageth not a fewe
from goyng to their bookes. Whereby learning greatlie decaieth, and barbarisme I
feare me will ouerflow the realme if speedie
remedie be not had herein.

Theod.   As farre as I can gather by
your speeches, there is both a reading and a
preaching ministerie, whether doe you prefer
before the other.

Amphil.   I preferre the preaching ministerie before a reading ministerie only: and yet
the reading ministerie if the other can not be
had, is not therefore euill, or not necessarie.

Theod. But tell me this. If there might a
preaching ministerie be gotten ought not the
reading ministerie to giue place to the same?

Amphil. Yea, doubtlesse. And therfore the
bishops ought to seeke for the learned sort, and
as it were to sue and make instance to them,
and finding them worthy as well for their life,
as doctrine to call them lawfully according to
the prescript of Gods word, & so to sende them
forth into the Lords haruest . And where the
foresaide dumbe ministerie is , to displace the
same, and place the other. By this meanes the

word

word of God should flourish, ignorance (maugger the head of satan) be abandoned, the church edified, and manie a one incouraged to go to their bookes, whereas now they practise nothing lesse, and all by reason that by their learning they haue no promotion nor preferment at all.

Theod. Do these preaching ministers preach onely in their owne cures, flockes and charges, or else indifferently abroad else where?

Amphil. They preach for the most part in their owne charges, and cures whereouer the holie Ghost hath made them ouerseers, and for which they shall render a dreadfull account at the day of iudgemennt, if they doe not their dutie, diligently as God hath commanded. But though they preach most commonly in their owne cures, yet doe they sometimes helpe their felowe brethren to breake the bread of life to their charges also. Wherein me thinke they do not amisse. For if a watch man appointed by a whole citie, or towne to giue warning when the enimie commeth, seeing an other citye, or towne to be in danger, giueth sufficient warning to his owne citie, and goeth and warneth the other citie also, and so by this meanes deliuereth them both, I say, that in so doing, he doth well, and according to charitie. And yet notwith-

notwithstanding diuers new phangled felows sprong vp of late, as the Brownists, and there adherents, haue spoken verie blasphemouslie hereof, teaching in their railing pamphletes, that those who are lecturers or preach els wher than in their owne cures, are accursed before god. Than the which, what can be more absurdlie, or vntruely spoken? For if they grant (as they cannot deny) that the word of God is good, then cannot the declaration of that which is good in one place be hurtfull in another. And read we not that the apostles themselues went from place to place, preaching the word to euerie congregation? Christ Iesus did the same, & also taught vs, that he came not to preach to one citie onely, but to many?

Theod. Doe the reading ministers onely continue and read altogither in their owne charges or not?

Amphil. The reading ministers after they be hired of the parishes (for they are mercenaries) they read commonly in their owne charges, and cures, except (which is a horrible abuse) that they haue two or three cures to serue all vpon one day, and peraduenture two or three myles distant, one from another. Which maketh them to gallop it ouer, as fast as they can, and to chop it vp with all possible expedition,

on, though none vnderstand them, and as fewe
be edified by them.

Theod.   Bee these reading ministers well
prouided for, so as they want nothing, or
not?

Amphil   No truly. For if the other preaching ministers bee not well prouided for (as
in truth they be not) then how can the other be
well maintained? And therfore they haue some
of them ten pound a yeere. (which is the most)
some eight pound, some sixe pound, some fiue
pound, some foure pound, some fortie shillings,
yea and table themselues also of the same.
And sometimes failing of this too, they runne
roging like vagarents vp & downe the countries like maisterlesse men, to seeke their
maintenance. Whereby some fall to one mischiefe, some to another, to the great slander
of the Gospell of Iesus Christ, and scandall
of the godlie. And yet part of these reading
misters be too well prouided for, for some of
them haue two or three, yea foure or fiue benefices apeece, being resident but at one of
them at once, and peraduenture at neuer a
one, but raise it out elsewhere, purchasing a
dispensation for their discontinuance , and
then may no man say : Domine cur ita fa-
cis? Sir why doe you so? For hee hath
                                        plenarie

plenarie power and authozitie granted him so to doe.

Theod. That is an hozrible abuse that one man should haue two oz thzee, oz halfe a dozen benefices apeece as some haue, may anie man haue so many liuings at one time by the lawe of God, and good conscience?

Amphil. As it is not lawfull foz anie man to haue oz enioie two wiues at once, so is it not lawfull foz any man how excellent soeuer to haue mo benefices, mo flockes, cures, oz charges in his handes than one at once. Nay J am fullie persuaded that it is moze tollerable (and yet it is a damnable thing) foz a man to haue two wiues oz mo, than foz a man to haue two benefices at once oz mo. Foz by possibilitie a man might discharge the dutie of a good husband to two oz thzee wiues (yet to haue mo than one is the bzeach of Gods commandements) but no man though he were as learned as Saint Paule, oz the apostles themselues to whome were giuen supernaturall and extraozdinarie giftes and graces, is able sufficientlie to discharge his dutie in the instruction of one church, oz congregation, much lesse of thzee oz foure oz halfe a dozen as some haue. And as one father cannot bee manie fathers, one pastoz

manie

manie paſtours, noʒ one man diuerſe men,
ſo one ſheepeheard oʒ paſtour cannot, noʒ
ought not to haue diuers charges, and flocks at
once. Is it poſſible foʒ any ſhepheard though
he were neuer ſo cunning a man, to kæpe two
oʒ thʒæ flocks oʒ mo at once, and to ſæd them
wel and in due ſeaſon doing the dutie of a god
ſhepheard in euerie reſpect, they being diſtant
from him, ten, twentie, foʒtie, ſixtie, an hundʒed. two hundʒed, oʒ thʒæ hundʒed miles?
Much leſſe is there any man able to diſcharge
the dutie of a god paſtoʒ ouer ſo manie flocks,
churches, and congregatious ſo farre diſtant in
place, wheras the ſimpleſt flocke that is, requireth a whole, and perfect man, & not a pæce of a
man. Therfoʒe I aduiſe al beneffice mongers, &
haue mo charges then one, to take hæde to thei
ſelues, and to leaue them in time, foʒ the blod
of al thoſe within their cures, oʒ charges, that
die ghoſtlie, foʒ want of the truth of Gods
woʒd pʒeached vnto them, ſhall be poinʒed vpon their their heads, at the day of iudgement,
and be required at their hands.

   Theod.   If they haue ſo many beneffices a
pæce, and ſome ſo farre diſtant from another,
then it is not poſſible that they can be reſident
bpon them all at once. But the matter is in
diſpute, whether they may not as well be ab-
                      ſent,

sent, oz present, what is your iudgment of that?

Amphil. To doubt whether the pastoz ought
to be resident with his flocke, is to doubt whether the soule should be in the bodie, the eie in
the head, oz the watchman in his tower. Foz
this I am fully persuaded of, that as the soule
is the life of the bodie, and the eie the light of
the same, so the word of God preached is the
life, and light as well to the bodie as to the
soule of man. And as necessarie as the one is
to the bodie, so (and much moze) necessarie is
the other both to soule and bodie. Now certein
it is, these things cannot be applied without
the presence of the preacher oz pastoz, and therfoze is his absence from his flocke a dangerous
and a perilous thing, and as it were a taking
away of their life and light from them; which
commeth by the preaching of Gods word vnto
them.

Theod. But they say though they be not present by themselues, yet be they present by their
substitutes and deputies, is not that a sufficient discharge foz them befoze God?

Amphil. I grant they are present by their
deputies and substitutes, but if a man shoulde
loke into a great sozt of them, he should finde
them such as are fitter to feed hogs, than chzistian soules. Foz as foz some of them are they

not such as can scarcely read true english? And
for their zeale to Gods worde and true religion, are they not such as can scarce tell what it
meaneth ? The truth of Gods word they cannot easily preach nor expound. The aduersarie
they cannot refell : barke against sinne they
dare not , bicause their liues are licentious.
They will read you their seruice faire and
cleanly (as the doting papists did their blasphemous masses out of their portesses) and
when they haue done, they will to all kinde of
wanton pastimes and delights, with come that
come will, and that vpon sabboth day, festiuall
day, or other, no day is amisse to them. And all
the weeke after, yea all the yeere (if I said all
the yeeres of their life I lied not) they will not
sticke to keepe companie at the alehouse from
morning till night, tipling and swilling till
the signe be in Capricornus . Insomuch as if
you would know where the best cup of drinke
is, go to these malt wormes, and I warran
you you shall not misse of your purpose . Bi
these mercenaries their deputies, and the like
I grant they are present in all their flocks, bu
so as it were better, or as good they were ab
sent for any good they doe, but rather hurt b
their euill example of life . The residence o
these their deputies is no discharge for the
beso

before the tribunall seate of God: for notwith standing the same, let them be sure to answere for the bloud of euerie one of their sheepe, that miscarrieth through their default, or their deputies. Their deputies shal not excuse them at the day of iudgement I dare be their warrant. Therefore I wish them to take heed to it be time, least afterward it be too late.

Theod. But I heare say, that what is wan ting either in their deputies, or in themselues for not being daily resident, they supply either by preaching their quarter sermons themselues, or else (if they be not able) by procuring of o thers to do it for them. Is not that wel?

Amphil. It is as though a man euery quarter of a yeere once, should take his plow, & go draw a furrow in a field, & yet notwithstanding should looke for increase of the same: were not he a foo lish husbandman that wold do thus? And euen so is he no lesse vnwise that plowing but one furow, that is, preaching but one poore sermon in a quarter of a yeere (& perchance but one in a whole yeere, nay in 7. yeeres) wil notwithstan ding looke for gret increase of the same. Now the cause why this ground bringeth not forth fruit is, for that it is not plowed, furowed, & tilled al togither as it ought to be. So the cause where fore the poore churches doe not bring forth fruit

is, for that they are not furrowed, manured,
and tilled, as they ought, and bicause the word
of God is not preached vnto them, and as it
were braied, punned, interpreted, and expoun-
ded, ý it sinking down into the good ground of
their harts, might bring forth fruit to eternal
life. If the strongest mans body that liueth vpon the earth should be nourished with nothing
for a whole quarter of a yeeres space, but onely with two or three drops of aqua vite, aqua
angelica, or the like, euery day, and at euery
quarters end should be fed with all manner of
dainties, I am perswaded that his bodie notwithstanding would soone be weake inough.
Nay do you thinke it were possible to liue one
quarter of a yeere? Euen so falleth out in this
case. For although our soules (which liue by
the word of God, as our bodies doe by meate)
be daily fedde with hearing the word read as
it were with aqua vite, or sweet necter, and at
euerie quarters ende, haue a most excellent t
sumptuous banquet to pray vpõ, yet may they
macerate and pyne away notwithstanding for
lacke of the continuance of the same. And therfore the worde of God is to be preached night
and day, in time, and out of time, in season, and
out of season, and that without ceasing, or in-
termission. And if that saieng of the prophet be
true

true (as without all controuersie it is most true(that he is accursed. Qui fecerit opus do-mini negligenter, That doth the worke of the Lord negligently, or fradulently, then must it needs be, that those who hauing cure of soules, and doe seldome, or neuer preach, are within the compasse of this curse. Let them take heede to it. The apostle Paule said of himselfe, Væ mihi nisi euangelizauero, Wo be to me, if I preach not the gospel, and doe they thinke that the same wo is not proper to them if they preach not? Haue they a greater priuiledge than the blessed apostle saint Paule had? No, no, these vaine excuses will not serue them, therfore as they tender the saluation of their owne soules, and many others, I wish them to take heede, and to shew themselues painefull laborers in the Lords haruest.

Theod. As far as I remember by the lawes of Dnalgne there is a restraint, that none shall haue no more benefices at once than one, how is it then, that they can holde so manie a peece, without danger of the law?

Amphil. They make the lawes(as it were) shipmens hoosen, or as a nose of waxe, turning and wresting them, at their pleasure to anie thing they lust. But because they will auoide the lawes, they purchase a dispensation a ti-

L.3. cence,

cence, a commiffion, a pluralitie, a qualifica
tion, and J cannot tell what elfe, by vertu
whereof they may hold torquots fo manie, how
manie foeuer, and that with as good a confci
ence as Iudas receiued the mony for the which
he fold Chriſt Ieſus the Sauiour of the worlo
Or if this way will not ſerue, then get they to
be chaplines, to honorable, & noble perſonages
by prerogatiue whereof they may holde I can
not tell how manie benefices, yea as manie as
they can get. But I maruell whether they
thinke that theſe licenſes ſhall go for good pai
ment at the daie of iudgement. I thinke not
For ſure I am that no licenſe of man can diſ
penſe with vs, to doe that thing, which is a
gainſt Gods worde (as theſe totquots is) and
therfore vnlawful. They may blind the fooliſh
worlo with pretenſed diſpenſations, and qua
lifications, but the Lorde will bring them to
account for it in his good time, G D D grant
they may looke to it?

Theod.   In whome doth the patronage,
right, and gifture of theſe eccleſiaſtical promo
tions, and benefices conſiſt, in the churches
themſelues, or in whom elfe?

Amphil.   Indeede you ſaie well. For who
ſhoulde haue the patronage, the right, the in
tereſt, and gifture of the benefices, but the
churches

churches themselues, whose the benefices are by right, and to whome Proprio iure, They doe apperteine? For doe not the benefices consist either in tithes, or contributions, or both? Nowe, who giueth both the one and the other? Doe not the Churches? Then by good reason ought they to haue the gifture and bestowing of them, and the right and interest thereof ought to remaine in the power of the church, and not in anie other priuate man whatsoeuer.

      Theod.   Why? Then I perceiue you would not haue anie priuate or singuler man of what degree soeuer, to haue the patronage the right, or gifture of anie ecclesiasticall liuing, but the churches themselues, is not that your meaning?

  Amphil.   Yes truely, that is my meaning, and so I am of opinion it ought to be.

      Theod.   Why so I beseech you?

  Amphil.   Bicause one man may easely be corrupted, and drawne to bestowe his benefice eyther for fauour, affection, or monie, vppon such as bee vnworthie, the whole Church will not so. Againe, the whole liuing is nothing else but either pure almes, or deuotion, or both, the Gentelman or other that pretendeth the gifture thereof,

        giueth

giueth not the whole liuing himselfe, ergo hee
ought not to haue in his owne power, the only
gifture of the same. Thirdly the whole church
will not giue the same for simonie, one priuate
man may be induced to doe it. Fourthlie, the
church will kéepe no part of the liuing backe
from the pastor, if he doe his dutie, nor imploie
it to ther owne vse, the singularitie of one man
may easilie be abused : nay the most patrones
kéepe the fattest morsels to themselues, and
giue scarcely the crums to their pastors. But
if the benefice be woorth two hundred pound,
the will scarcely giue their pastor foure score.
If it be woorth an hundred pound, they will
hardly giue fortie pound. If woorth forty pound
it is well, if they giue ten pound, imploieng the
better halfe to their owne priuate gaine. Now
if this be not sacrilege, and a robbing of the
poore churches of their substance, as also a de-
frauding of the Lords minister of his dutie and
right, then I knowe not what sacrilege, and
fraude meaneth . Yea there are some, that hauing ground in another parish, than where
they dwell, against the time that their shéepe,
kine, and other cattell should bring foorth increase, will driue them thither, so that the fruit
falling in the other parish, he shall not néed to
pay tithes for the same to his owne pastor
                                    where

where he dwelleth. And against the time that the other pastor of that parish where his cattell fell, shall demand his tithes thereof, they will haue fetched home their cattell, so that by these sinister kind of meanes, they will neither pay in the one parish, nor in the other. But if the one commence sute against him, he answereth, they fell not in his parish: if the other doe the same, he pleadeth that he is not of his parish, nor oweth him ought. But indeed they wil pay for their ground in the other parish a little herbage (as they call it) a thing of nothing to stop his mouth withall. So that hereby the poore pastors are deteined from their right, and almost beggered in most places that I haue come in.

Theod. How came temporall men by the right of their patronages, and how fell they into their clowches, can you tell?

Amphil. I will tell you as farre as euer I could coniecture how they fel into their hands. In the beginning when Antichrist the pope exercised his vsurped authoritie, and challenged the title of supreme head ouer the vniuersall church of Christ vpon the face of the earth, to whomsoeuer would either erect churches, temples, and oratories (as then the world was giuen to blinde superstition as to instaurate abbeies,

beies, prieries, nunries, (with other sumptuous edefices, and houses of religion, thinking the same a worke meritorious, and to gilts, crosses images, and the like fooleries) or else giue ground for the same to be built vpon, his vnholie holines, did giue the patronage, and pretensed right of the same church, and benefice belonging to the same . Othersome thinke (to whome I willinglie subscribe) that the Churches (consisting of simple, and ignorant men for the most part) abusing the same benefices, and bestowing them vpon vnmeete persons, the princes haue taken them out of their handes, and giuen the right patronage, and possession of the same to the temporaltie, to the ende they might bestowe them better. But as they were taken from the churches for some causes, so ought they to be remooued and giuen againe to the Churches for greater causes. For nowe are they bought and soulde for simonie, euen as an ore or a cow is bought and sold for mony.

    Theod.   Are there no lawes for the restrainte of simonie, being so horrible, and detestable a vice in the church of God?

    Amphil. Yes that there are. As he that is patrone taking monie for his benefice, to loose the patronage of the same, and the

eccles.

ecclesiasticall person, that giueth it, to lose
the same benefice, the monie giuen o2 p2o-
mised to be giuen, and to remaine incapable
of anie other ecclesiasticall p2omotion after-
warde fo2 euer. But doe you thinke they
are fooles? Haue they no shift to defeate the
lawe. Yes I warrant you. Fo2 though they
giue two hund2ed, o2 th2ee hund2ed pound fo2
a benefice, yet it shall be done so closely, as
no dogges shall barke at it. But bicause at the
time of their initiation, institution, induction,
and admission they are swo2ne whether they
came by it by simonie o2 no, whether they
gaue anie monie fo2 it, o2 no, therefo2e to a-
uoide the guilte of periurie, they the pasto2s
themselues will not giue anie monie, but
their friendes shall doe it fo2 them, and than
may they sweare (with as good a conscience
as euer Iudas betraied Ch2ist) that they
gaue not a penny, but came by it freely, as
of gifte. O2 if this waie fayle them, than
must they giue the patrones a hund2ed
pounde, o2 two hund2ed pounds vpon some
bargayne, that is not woo2th a hund2ed
pence, and then maye they sweare if nede
be, that they came by the benefice franke-
lye, and freelye, and that they gaue the
money vpon such and such a bargaine,
                                    without

without ſome of theſe practiſes , or without
ſuch a diſh of apples, as Maſter Latimer talk-
eth of with thirty angels in euery apple, thogh
he be neuer ſo learned a man, I warrant him,
he gets nothing. But if he can get a graffe of
this tree loden with ſuch golden apples, it will
ſerue him better, then all Saint Paules learning. For theſe and the like abuſes infinite , if
the patronages were taken away from them,
that now enioy them, nay, that make hauocke
of them , and either to reſt in the right of the
Prince (as they ought) or elſe in the right of
the churches, who will not be corrupted , it
were a great deale better, than nowe they bee.
For now the poore paſtours are ſo handled at
the hands of their patrones, that they neyther
haue mony to buy them bookes withall, nor
which is leſſe not to maintaine themſelues
vppon though but meanelye, but are manye
times conſtrained either to wander abroad to
ſæke their liuings or els to take vp their Inne
in an alehouſe, or in ſome od corner or other,
to the great diſcredite of the goſpell of Chriſt,
and offence of the goodlie. This argueth flatly
that we loue not Chriſt Jeſus , who make ſo
little of his meſſengers, and ambaſſadors. He
that deſpiſeth you, deſpiſeth me, and he that re-
ceaueth and maketh much of you, he receiueth
me,

me, and maketh much of me saith Chrift. The
heathen gentils, and pagans, prouide better
for their idolatrous priefts, then we do for the
true preachers of the gospell, and disclofers of
the secrets of God. For when the Egyptians
were fore pooled of Pharao, the priefts by his
commandement were excepted, and permitted
to haue all necessarie maintenance whatsoeuer. But we are of another mind, for we think
whatsoeuer we get of thē is won, it is our own
good, whereas in truth, what we withdrawe
from thē (prouided that they be diligent preachers of the pospell we withdraw it frō God,
and ferrie it to the deuil. But hereof more shal
be spoken (Chrift willing) hereafter, when we
come to this question, whether it be lawful for
preachers and miniffers of the Gospell, to receiue wages and ftipends for preaching of the
worde.

Theod. By what law may a miniffer of the
Gospell make claime to tithes, and other profits, emoluments, duties and commodities, belonging to him, by þ law of God, or of man?

Amphil. God in the law of Moses, gaue speciall commandement that tithes, and other
oblations, commodities, and profits should be
giuen to the priefts, to the end that they might
attend vpon the diuine feruice of God, and not
                                                            busie

busie themselues in worldly affaires, which ordinance or sanction being méere ceremonial, is now fully abrogate by Christ (for in him the truth, al ceremonies, shadowes, types & figures ceased, & toke their end.) And therfore cannot a preacher of the Gospel claime his tithes by the lawe of Moses, but by the positiue lawes of Christian princes, which are to be obeied in all things (not directly against true godlinesse) vpon paine of damnation.

Theod. Are tithes then due to be paid by the positiue law of man, and not by the lawe of God?

Amphil. Yea truly by the positiue lawe of man: which godlie constitution is now no lesse to be obeied vnder the Gospel (being commanded by a christian prince) than the diuine institution was to be obeied vnder the law. And although tithes bee due by the positiue lawes of man, yet are the same grounded vpon the word of God, and commanded as well by God as by man. And therefore he that breaketh this ordinance (being an excellent policie) violateth the commandements of God, and breketh the constitution of his liege prince to his damnation, except he repent.

Theod. Must euerie one pay his tithes truely to euery pastor whether he be ought, or naught

naught, learned o2 vnlearned, without any exception, o2 may he deteine it with god conscience from him that is an vnfit and vnable minister?

Amphil. If he be a god pasto2 and diligent in his calling, and withal able to discharge the dutie of a faithful shepheard ouer his flock, then ougtt he to haue al tithes paid him whatsoeuer with the better, and if any should withhold the left mite from him, he sinneth against the maiestie of God most gréeuously. And although he be a wicked man, and not able to discharge his dutie, though but in small measure, yet ought euerie man to pay him his due faithfully and truly. Fo2 in denieng him his dutie, they might séeme to withstande autho2itie, which they ought not to doe. In the meane time giuing themselues to p2aier, and suing to them that haue the autho2itie fo2 his displacing, and placing of another that is mo2e able in some measure to discharge the dutie of a faithfull pasto2. Notwithstanding I know some are of opinion that if any man giue either tithes, o2 anie dutie else to their pasto2 being an vnfit, and an vnable person, he is partaker with him of his sinne, he communicateth with other mens offences, and he maintaineth him in his idlenesse, sloth, igno2ance,

and

and securitie, and therefore offendeth grǽuou-
sly. But I am of opinion that euerye man
ought to pay their dutie (for else he might sǽme
as I said to resist the power) & if he be not able
to discharge his dutie, to pray for his remo-
uing, and to make instance to them that are in
authoritie appointed for the redresse of such in-
ormisies, for his displacing, and so not to at-
temot any thing without good and lawfull authoritie grounded vpon the word for the same.

Theod. May a pastor that hath a charge and
a flocke assigned him to watch ouer (hauing a
maintainable liuing allowed him of his flock)
preach in other places for monie?

Amphil. Yee may sometimes obteining licence for some reasonable cause of his owne
flocke, preach the word of God abroad in other
places, but then he ought to doe it gratis, contenting himselfe with the liuing allowed him
at home of his owne parish. Notwithstanding,
if the other churches where he shall haue preached, will voluntarily impart any thing to the
supplie of his necessities, in respect of his pains
taking, he may thankfully receine the same,
but he may not compell, nor constraine them
to giue it him whether they will or not againe
their wils, as manie impudently do.e

Theod. Then I perceiue if it be not lawfull

full for a pastor that hath a flocke, and a stipend appointed him, to receiue monie vppon constraint of strangers for preaching the worde abroad in other places, then is it not lawfull for him to take monie in his cure for preaching funerall sermons, marriage sermons, christening sermons, and the like, as many do. What say you to this?

Amphil. There are manie worthie of great blame in this respect. For though they receiue fortie pound, a hundred pound, or two hundred pound a yeere, of some one parish, yet will they hardly preach once a moneth, nay happily not once in a quarter of a yeere, and sometimes not once a twelue moneth, for the same. And if a man request them to preach at a burial, a wedding, or a christening, they will not doe it vnder an angell, or a noble at the lest. And therefore the papists, and aduersaries to the Gospel call our Gospel, a polling Gospel, our sermons roiall sermons, angell sermons, and noble sermons. You call say they our blessed masse a polling masse, but say they your preachings are more polling. For we say they would haue sold a masse for a grote, you will not sell a sermon vnder a roiall, or a noble. And thus these fellowes are a slander to the Gospel, and robbers of their fellowe brethren. If I should hire a

M.I.   man

man for fortie pound, an hundred pound, or
more, or lesse, to teach my children nurture and
knowledge, if he for the execution therof should
aske me more for the same than we agreed for,
were not this man a naughtie, exacting, and
fraudulent felowe? Nay if I compound with
him to teach them in the best maner he is able
for so much, and he doth it not, and yet receiue
my monie, haue not I good lawe against him?
If he should say vnto me, I will not doe it except you giue me more, were not this a very
vnreasonable man? For hauing his monie
that was couenant, is hee not bound both by
lawe and conscience to teach them to the vttermost of his power? Or if he shall not doe it,
and yet take my monie, is not he a theefe and a
robber? Is this true in a priuate man, & not in
an ecclesiasticall person? Is he not hired to that
end & purpose to preach the word of God to his
flocke? And hath hee not wages for the same?
Shall he now denie to preach the same word
except he haue more monie? Or is he not bound
in conscience to preach the same night and day
without ceasing? And if he doe not, is he not a
deceiuer, a theefe, & a robber? The pastor therefore hauing taken vpon him the cure & charge
of his flocke, and hauing his stipend appointed
for the same, is bound to preach the worde of
God

God to all his flocke indifferently whether it be at buriall, wedding, christening (yea then especially) oz at any other time whensoeuer, without taking, oz requiring of any moze mo=nie, than the stipend he was hired foz. Foz if he take any moze, it is plaine theft befoze God, and one day shall be answered foz : let them be sure of it.

Theod. Pou condemne not funerall sermons then, so that they be good, doe you ?

Amphil. Po, God fozbid. Why should not godlie sermons be as wholsome (and as neces=sarie) at the burials of christians, when wee haue such liuely spectacles befoze our eies, of our moztalitie, miserie, and end, as they be at all other times ? Pea truely at that pzesent I thinke godlie sermons verie necessarie to put the people in remembzance of their moz=talitie, of their great miserie, and frailtie, of their fatall end, of the immoztalitie of the soule, of the generall resurrection at the last day, and of the ioie, felicitie, and beatitude of the life to come, with the like godlie in=structions, that they may the better pzepare themselues to the same when God shall call them hence to himselfe . And although of late some phantasticall spirites haue taught that the vse of them is naught, in that they

stand

stand in place of popish diriges, and I cannot tell what, yet cannot I be easilie drawne to assent vnto them, for that I sée them in that respect a great deale more curious than godlie wise.

Theod. Is it lawfull thinke you for ministers, and preachers of the Gospell to receiue stipends, and wages for their preaching?

Amphil. Why not? Otherwise how should they bee able to kéepe themselues frée from worldly occupations, and trauels of this life (as they ought) to applie their studies for the discharge of their duties, to maintaine themselues, their family, and houshold, or how shuld they kéepe hospitalitie for the reléefe of the poore, all which they are bound to doe both by Gods lawe, and good conscience? Therefore take away liuings, and wages from the preachers, and ouerthrowe preaching altogither, the ordinarie meane to saluation in Christ. This caused the apostle to enter disputation of this point, where he proueth by inuincible arguments, that a preacher or minister of the Gospell of Christ Iesus, may (Salua conscientia, With a good conscience) receiue wages, and stipends for his paines susteined in the affaires of the Gospell, and that for the causes abouesaid. Therefore saith this apostle: Boui trituranti

trituranti non ligabis os, Thou shalt not muffle the mouth of the oxe that treadeth foorth the corne. Whereby is ment, that he that laboreth, and taketh paines in any good exercise, ought not to be denied of his meed for his paines. Againe he saith : Dignus est operarius mercede sua, The workman is worthie of his reward. And still insisting in the same argument, hee saith : Qui euangelium prædicant, ex euangelio viuant, They that preach the Gospell, let them liue vpon the Gospell. And yet further prosecuting the same more at large, he saith : Quis militat, &c. Who goeth on warfare at any time of his owne charges? Who planteth a vineyard, and eateth not of the fruit? Who fædeth a flocke, and eateth not of the milke of the flock. By al which reasons, and arguments it appeareth, that he who preacheth the Gospel ought to liue of the Gospell. But as euerie pastor that hath a peculiar flocke assigned him may with the testimonie of a good conscience receiue wages, and maintenance of his flocke, for his paines taken amongst them : so may he not, nor ought not to take wages or salarie of any other flocke adioining, if so be it, that either vpon request, or his owne voluntarie good will, he preach the word of God amongst them. To them that are thus prouided for, Christ our

sauiour.

sauiour saith : Gratis accepistis, gratis date,
Freely you haue receiued, freely giue againe.
But if any haue not a speciall flocke, or charge
assigned him, then may he with good conscience receiue the beneuolencie, the friendly
contributions, and rewards of the churches to
whom he hath preached . And this is probable
both by the word of God, and the examples of
the apostles themselues.

Theod. What say you of preachers, and
lecturers, that haue no peculiar flockes, nor
charges appointed them, are they necessarie,
and may they receiue wages with a good conscience of the flockes, and charges where they
preach the word of God?

Amphil. First you aske me whether preachers , and lecturers that haue no peculiar
flocks nor charges of their owne to attend vp-
en, be necessarie. Whereto I answere. That
considering the state, & condition of the church
at this day, they are most necessarie. But if it
were so, that euerie church and congregation
had his preacher (as euery one ought to preach,
else is he not sent by the Lord) then were they
not so necessarie , but considering that most
churches are planted and fraught with single
reading ministers, they are very behouefull
to helpe to supplie the defect of the others, that
through

through the good industrie as well of the one, as of the other, the churches of GOD may bee instructed and nourished with the worde of GOD to eternall life. Then you aske mee whether these lecturers and preachers may receiue wages of the churches to whom they preach, with a good conscience, whereto I answere, that they may. But yet I am persuaded, that it were much better for them to haue particular flocks of their owne. to the end that they receiuing sufficient maintenance of them, might (if they were at anie time disposed to bestowe any spirituall graces abroad) doe it Gratis, frankly and freely without any charges to the poore churches of Jesus Christ.

Theod. But what if the pastors liuing be not maintaineable nor sufficient for him to liue vpon, may hee not take wages of other flocks abroad?

Amphil. I am persuaded no. For if his liuing be to little, then ought the church to mend it, but if the church either for want of zeale will not, or through extreame pouertie cannot increase his liuing, then ought the pastor to content himselfe with that little, which God hath sent him, following the example of the apostle, who biddeth the children of GOD

to

to bee content with their wages, bee it little or be it much: for if they haue meate, drinke, and cloth, it is inough, and as much as nature requireth. We brought nothing (saith he) into this world, neither shall we carrie any thing out Againe, those that will be rich, fall into diuers temptations, and snares of the diuell, which drowne men in perdition and destruction. Therefore if it be sufficient to yeelde him meate, drinke, cloth, and other necessaries, he is bound to content himselfe with the same. Which if he doe (for the zeale he beareth to his flocke) I doubt not but the Lord will open the harts of his flock towards him, and both make them able, and willing to support his necessities. For if hee deliuer vnto them spirituall things, doubtlesse the Lord will moue them to giue vnto him temporall things. And therfore ought he to perseuere, and in his good time, without all peraduenture the Lord will looke vpon him, as he hath promised.

Theod. Doe you allow of that vagarant ministerie, which is in manie countries, but most specially in Dnalgne sprong vp of late, to the discredite of the Gospell of Jesus Christ, and offence of the brethren?

Amphil. Allow of it quoth you? No God forbid. But I rather deplore it with all my hart, knowing

knowing that it is most directly against the
word of God, the example of the primitiue age,
and all good reformed churches thorough the
world. Is it not a pitifull case that two hundred, three hundred, fiue hundred, a thousand,
fiue thousand, yea possible ten thousand shall
be called into the ministerie, in one countrie,
not a quarter of them knowing where to haue
any liuing or charge? And what do they then?
Runne stragling, and rouing ouer countries,
from towne to towne, from citie to citie, from
shire to shire, and from one place to another,
till they haue spent al that euer they haue, and
then the most of them either become beggers,
or else attempt wicked and vnlawfull meanes
to liue by, to the great dishonour of God, and
slander of the word.

Theod. Me thinke this is a great abuse, that
so manie, or any at all should be called into the
ministerie, not hauing flocks, and charges prouided for them before.

Amphil. It is a great abuse indeed. For if
pastor come of Pasco, to fæd, if he be not a shepheard that hath no flock, and if he be not a fee-
der, that giueth no sustinance, nor a father that
hath no childe, then are they no shepheards, nor
no watchmen sent from the Lord, that haue
neither flocks, nor charges to watch ouer. For
be

he that is made a shepheard (or a minister) that hath no particular flocke readie to receiue him, is so far from being a lawfull shepheard, by reason of his former admission, that he is rather made a pastor by the church that hireth him to be their watchman and guide, than of him that first called him into that function. And therefore woulde I wish that bishops and others to whome it doth (Ex officio) apperteine to call, and admit pastors, and teachers in the church of G O D, to bee verie carefull héerein, and not rashly to lay their handes vpon any, before they haue had sufficient triall as well of their life and doctrine, as also of the flock and charge where they shal be resident, that they go not like maisterlesse hounds vp and downe the countries to the slander of the Gospell.

Theod. Why? Then I perceiue you would haue none called into the ministerie, before there be a place void for him, is not that your meaning?

Amphil. That is my meaning indéed.

Theod. But are you able to proue your assumption, out of the word of God, or else I will giue but small credit to you in such matters of controuersie as this is?

Amphil.

Amphil. I haue not, neither doe I meane to speake anie thing vnto you touching these matters, but what I am able (I trust) to proue by the worde of GOD. And yet I grant Errare possum (for Hominis est labi, & decipi, Man may bee deceiued and fall) but Hereticus esse nolo, Erre I may, but heretike I will not be. No, so soone as I shall be conuinced by the manifest worde of God, of any of my former positions or assertions, I will willingly subscribe to the truth. But being persuaded as I am, giue me leaue, I beseech you (vnder correction) to speake what I thinke. But now to the purpose. In the first chapter of the Actes of the apostles recorded by the Euangelist Saint Luke, wee read that Matthias succeeding Iudas the traitour in the administration of the apostleship, was not chosen nor elected (notwithstanding that the apostles by the reuelation of the spirite of GOD, knew that he should fall from the same in the end) vntill the place was voide, and emptie. In the sixt chapter of the Actes of the apostles wee reade also of seuen deacons, which were chosen for the dailie ministring to the poore, but when I pray you? Not before the church (destitute of their seruice) had need of them, nor before there were

were places readie to receiue them, wherein
they might exercise their function, and calling.
Then if the apostles would not chose not so
much as deacons, which is an office in the
church of God farre inferiour to the office of
the pastor, or preacher, before places were void
and readie to receiue them, much lesse would
they, or did they chose or call any pastor into
the church of God, before the church stood in
need of him, and before there be a place readie
to receiue him. Besides that, we read not thorough the whole euangelicall historie, that
euer the apostles called any to be pastors and
preachers of the word, before such time as there
we places void for them. Common reason
me inke, and daily experience should teach
vs th 3 truth sufficiently, if we were not wil-
fully blinded, that when any church or congregation is destitute of a pastor, it were better to
place there one able person, than to make two
or three hundred, or mo vnable sellowes, and
they for want of liuing to runne stragling the
countries ouer, without any liuing or maintenance at all, being glad of any thing. For as
the old saieng is : Hungrie dogs eate sluttish
puddings.

    Theod. What order would you haue obser-
ued in this ?

                             Amphil,

Amphil. Me thinke this were a verie good order. That euerie church or congregation being destitute of a pastor should present to the bishops, and others to whom it dooth appertaine, one or two, three or foure able persons, or mo, or lesse, as they conueniently can, whose liues and conuersations they haue had sufficient triall of, whose soundnesse in religion, integritie of life, and godly zeale to the truth they are not ignorant of. Then the bishops and others to whom it doth apperteine, to examine and trie them thoroughly for their sufficiencie in learning, soundnesse in doctrine, and dexteritie in teaching, and finding them furnished with sufficient gifts for such an honorable calling to admit them, to lay their hands vppon them, and to send them foorth (the chiefest of them) to that congregation or church so destitute. Which order if it were strictly obserued and kept (as it ought to be) then should not so manie run abroad in the countries to seeke liuings, then should not churches bee pestered with insufficient ministers. Then should not the bishops be so deceiued in manie as they be. And no maruell. For how should the bishop choose but be deceiued in him, whom he neuer sawe before, whose conuersation he knoweth not, whose disposition hee is ignorant of, and

whose

whose qualities and properties in generall, he suspecteth not? Whereas if this order were established, that euerie church destitute of a pastor should present certeine able men, whose conuersation and integritie of life in euerie respect they perfectly knowe (for the whole church is not likely to erre in iudging of their conuersations, who haue béene either altogither, or for the most part conuersant amongst them) then (as I say, should not the bishop be deceiued in any, nor yet any church scandalized with the wicked liues of their pastors (or rather depastors) as they be. For now it is thought sufficient for the certeintie of his conuersation, if he either haue letters dimissorie from one bishop to another (whereas they little or nothing knowe the conuersation of the man) or else letters commendatorie from any gentleman, or other, especially if they be of any reputation. If he can get these things, he is likely to spéede I warrant him. Which thing is scarce well in my iudgement. For you knowe one priuate man, or two, or thrée, or foure may peraduenture either write vpon affection, or else bee corrupted with bribes or gifts, whereas the whole church can not, nor would not. Therefore is the other the surer way.

Theod

Theod. How proue you that the chur-
ches that are destitute of a pastor, ought to present him whom they would haue admitted, to
the bishop, and not the bishop to intrude vpon
the church whom he will?

Amphil. In the first chapter of the Actes
of the apostles before cited, we read, that after
the defection of Iudas the traitour, the apostle
Peter knowing it necessarie that one shoulde
be chosen in his place, to giue testimonie and
witnesse of the resurrection, and ascension
of Christ Iesus, commanded the church to
present one or two, or mo, as they thought
good, that hee with his fellowe brethren
might confirme and allow them. And there-
vppon saith the text, they chose two, to wit,
Matthias, and Ioseph, surnamed Bersabas.
And the church hauing presented them, they
were elected, confirmed, and allowed of the
apostles and elders. Also in the foresaide first
chapter of the Acts of the apostles when the
deacons (whose office was to make collections
for the poore, and to see the same bestowed vpon
them without fraud or deceit) were to be chosen, the text saith, that the apostles desired the
church to chose forth seuen men from amongst
them, of honest report, & ful of the holie Ghost,
which they might appoint to that businesse.

By

By all which reasons appereth, that the church ought to present him, or them, whom they would haue to be admitted, and not that the bishop ought to present, to allow, or to intrude him vpon the church at his pleasure against the will thereof.

Theod. Why would you not haue pastors to be thrust vpon the churches, whether the churches will or not?

Amphil. Bicause it is manifest that no church will so willingly receiue, nor yet so louingly imbrace him that is intruded vpon them against their wils, as they will doe him that they like of, choose, and allow of themselues. And if the churches beare not a singular loue, fauour, good will, and affection to their pastor, it is vnpossible that they should heare him, or learne of him with profit to their soules. And if they heare him not Auide & sitienter (as we say) Greedily and thirstily thereby to profit, then shal they perish euerlastingly, in that the word of God is the ordinarie meane appointed by the diuine maiestie. And therefore in conclusion if there be not a mutual amitie, loue, and affection betwixt the pastor and his flocke, and if that the one loue not the other, as themselues, it is not to be looked for that either the one shall teach, or the other receiue any thing to their soules health,

health, but rather the cleane contrarie.

Theod. J pray you what is your iudgement in this? What if a man be once lawfully called into the ministerie, may he euer vpon anie occasion whatsoeuer, leaue off the same function, and applie himselfe to secular affaires?

Amphil. There is a twofold calling. The one a diuine calling immediately from God, the other a humane calling immediately from and by man. Now he that hath the first diuine calling (his conscience suggesting the same vnto him, and the spirit of God certifieng his spirit of the certeintie thereof) being furnished with gifts and graces necessarie for such a high function and office (as God calleth none, but he indueth them first with gifts, and graces necessarie for their calling) and afterwards is lawfully called of man according to the prescript of Gods word, hauing a flocke appointed him wherevpon to attend, this man may not, nor ought not at any hand to giue ouer his calling, but to perseuere in the same to the end, for that he hath both the diuine and humane callings, being furnished with all gifts, and graces necessarie (in some measure) for the discharge of his high function and calling. Yet notwithstanding in time of extreame persecution, when Gods truth is persecuted, and his glorie defa-

ced,

red, if he haue not wherewithall to maintaine
his estate otherwise, he may for the time giue
himselfe to manuall occupations, and corporall exercises in the affaires of the worlde, as
we see the apostles themselues did, who after
Christ Iesus was crucified gaue themselues
to their old occupations of fishing, making of
of nets, tents, pauilions, and the like. But vpon the other side, if a man haue not this diuine
calling, his conscience bearing him witnesse
thereof, nor yet the graces, gifts, and orna-
ments of the minde, fit for his calling (which
whosoeuer hath not, it is a manifest argument
that the Lorde hath not sent him, for those
that hee sendeth, hee furnisheth with all kinde
of graces, and giftes necessarie for their callings) this man though he be called by humane
calling neuer so precisely, yet he may, nay hee
ought to leaue his function, as vnwoorthie
to occupie a roome in the church of God, repre-
senting (as an idoll doth) that thing which hee
is not. Besides, hee that is compelled, and
inforced either by friendes (as manie are)
or by pouertie (as not a few bee) or for anie
other respect else to take that high function
vpon him, without the testimonie of a good
conscience, being not furnished with gifts, and
graces fit for such a calling (which argueth directly

rectly that God hath not called him) hee I say is so farre from being bounde neuer to leaue his function and calling, that hee ought not one minute of an houre to continue in the same, though he bee called by man a thousande times. Therefore he that is a minister, and hath charge of soules committed vnto him, let him if hee bee not furnished with such gifts as his high calling requireth, in the name of GOD make no doubt of it to giue ouer his function vnto others that are able for their giftes to discharge the same, in the meane time giuing himselfe to godlie exercises of life, as God may be glorified, his conscience disburthened, and the commonwealth profited.

Theod. But I haue heard of some that considering the naughtinesse of their calling, and their owne insufficiencie to discharge the same, haue therefore left off their function, giuing themselues to secular exercises, and in the ende haue béene inforced to resume their former function vpon them againe, and that whether they would or not. How thinke you of this?

Amphil. I thinke truely that they who compelled them to take againe that function which they were not able to discharge, and

therefor

therefore left it haue grȩuously offended therein. This is as if I knowing a simple ignozant
fȯle pzesumptuously to haue taken vpon him
a great and waightie charge, yea such a charge
as all the wisedome in the wozld is not able
thozoughly to perfozme, and when he in taking
a biew of his owne insufficiencie, shuld be mo-
ued to leaue his charge to others better able to
execute the same than hee, I should notwithstanding not onely counsell, but also compell
him to resigne againe his fozmer great charge
which I knowe he is neither wozthie, noz yet
able euer to accomplish . Thinke you not that
he that compelleth him to take againe that office oz calling which befoze he had leaft foz
his inabilitie, shall not answere foz the same,
yes truely, you may be sure of it ? In conclusion, he that is sufficiently furnished with such
gifts as are necessarie foz his calling, & withal
is found able to discharge in some sozt his duty
ought not to leaue his function (foz to such a
on that so doth, Chzist saith hee that laieth
hande vpon the plough, and looketh backe, is
not fit foz the kingdome of God.) But againe,
he that hath not these gifts, and graces sufficient foz his calling, to the discharge of his dutie
ought not to occupie a place in the church of
God, as the pastoz thereof, much lesse ought he
when

when he hath (for his inabiltie) leaft the same to be constraied to resume againe his former function, and calling, which he is not able to discharge. But hereof inough.

Theod. Then I perceiue that any minister or ecclesiasticall person that hath not gifts sufficient to discharge his duty may with good conscience leaue their functions, and giue themselues to liue by their labors, as other temporall men doe, may they not?

Amphil. Yes, with a better conscience than to retaine them being not able to discharge them in any small measure. For with what conscience can he receiue temporall things of his flocke, and is not able to giue them spirituall? With what face can a shepeheard receiue of his sheepe, the milke, the wooll, and fleece, and yet will not, or cannot giue to the same either meate or drinke sufficiently? With what conscience can he receiue fortie pound, a hundred pound, or two hundred pound, a yeere of his poore flocke, and is not able to breake to them the breade of life, in such forme, and maner as he ought? Nay how can he euer haue quiet conscience that knowing that the blood of all those that die ghostlie for want of instruction shal be powred vpon his head at the day of iudgment, and be demanded at his handes, will yet not

P.3

with

notwithstanding reteane the same charge, and
function to himselfe still, not being able to discharge the least iote of the same? Therefore
would I wish euery man of what office, function, or calling soeuer he be, if he be not able to
discharge his dutie in the same, to giue it ouer,
and not for greedinesse of a little mucke or
dung of the earth, (for monie is no better) to
cast away their soules, which Iesus Christ
hath bought with his most precious blood.

Theod. Is it lawfull for a pastor or minister that hath a flocke to departe from the
same. In the time of plague, pestilence, or
the like, for feare of infection?

Amphil. Is he a good sheepeheard that
when he seeth the wolues comming, will take
him to his heeles and runne away? Or is he a
sure freend that when a man hath most neede
of his helpe, will then get him packing, not
shewing any freendship towardes him at all?
I thinke not? And truly no more is he a good
pastor, or minister, (but rather a depastor,
and minister) that in time of any plague pestilence or sicknes, whatsoeuer will conuey himselfe away from his flocke, for feare of infection, at the houre of death, when the poore people haue most need of comfort aboue all other
times, then is he their pastor that should feede
them,

them, the furthest from them. When they stande vppon the edge as it were of saluation, or damnation, then permits he the wolfe to haue the rule ouer them. Our Sauiour Christ saith Bonus pastor animulam dat pro ouibus, A good shepheard giueth his life for his sheepe, but these felowes are so far from giuing their liues for their sheepe, that they seeke to saue their owne liues with the destruction of their whole flocke. This is the loue that they beare vnto their flocke, this is the care they haue ouer their soules health, which Christ Iesus bought so deere with the price of his blood. Out vppon those shepheards that for feare of incurring of corporall death (which is to the Godly an entraunce into parpetuall glorie) will hazard manie a thousande to die a corporall and a spirituall death both, yea, a death of damnation both of body & soule for euer. Do they thinke that their blod shall not be asked at their hands at y̆ gret day of the Lord. Do they thinke y̆ their flieng away from their flock, is a mean to preserue their liues y̆ longer vpon earth: Is not God able to strike them as well in the fields, as in the city, as well in the country as in the towne, in one place, as well as in another? Is not his power euerie where? Is not his messenger death in al places? Saith he not in the boke of Deuteron. that if we doe

not

not thoſe things, which he hath commanded
vs in his ſacred word, curſed ſhall wee bee at
home, and curſed in the fields. And ſaith he not
further, that the plague and peſtilence, the
botch, bile, blaine, or elſe what deadly infection
ſoeuer ſhall followe vs, and lay hold vpon vs,
in what place ſoeuer we be, and ſhall neuer de-
part from vs, till it haue quite conſumed vs
from the face of the earth? And doe theſe fugi-
tiues that ouerrun their flocks in time of infection, thinke that they ſhall eſcape the heauie
wrath and vengeance of God for their tergi-
uerſation and backſliding from their duties?
Doe they thinke that God cannot ſaue them
frm corporal death, but with the breach of their
duties towards God? Is not the Lord as well
able to defend them from any deadly infection
if it be his good pleaſure, as he was to defend
Sidrach, Miſaach, and Abednego from the fla-
ming fire? Daniell from the mouth of the lions, Ionas frō the iawes of the mightie whale,
with manie others that truſted in him? Doe
they thinke that his arme is ſhortened, or his
power weakened? Is he not able to deliuer
his children, that in doeing of their duties depend vpon his prouidence? And to bee plaine
with them, me think that in fleeng away from
their flockes, they ſhew themſelues to thinke
that

that either God is not almightie, o2 else noe mercifull, o2 neither. Fo2 if they beleued that he were almightie, and that hee were able to saue them, then they would neuer run awaie from their flocke, but depending vpon his p2o-uidence, beleue that he is as well able to deli-uer them in one place as in another, if it bee his good pleasure. And if they beleued that he were mercifull, then would they rest vpon the same, not doubting, but as he is almightie, and omnipotent, and therefo2e can doe al things, so he is most mercifull, and therfo2e wil p2eserue al those that put their trust in him. If a tempo-rall magistrate that exerciseth but a ciuil office in the commonwealth shuld go away from his charge fo2 feare of infection o2 plague, wheras his p2esent abode might do mo2e good than his absence, he greatly offendeth, how much mo2e then offendeth he, that being a pasto2 o2 fæder of soules, flieth away from his charge, wheras his p2esence might doe a thousand times mo2e good than his absence? And if it please the Lo2d to take them away to himselfe, are they not most happie? Enter they not into eternal glo-rie? And haue they not an end of all miseries and paines in this life, and the perfect fruition of perpetuall ioie in the heauens? Are they not blessed, if when the Lo2d shal call them, he find

them

them so well occupied as in feeding, & breaking the bread of life to the poze members of Christ Iesus for whose sakes he shed his hart blood?

Theod. But they say, we ought not to tempt God, which thing they must needs doe if they should tarrie when they see death before their face. And they say further, that it is written that we must keepe the whole from the sicke, and the sicke from the whole. Besids saie they, Natura dedit, potestatem tuendi vitam omni animanti, Nature hath giuen power of defending of life to euerie liuing creture. Againe, euery thing fleeth from his contrarie, but death is contrarie to nature, for it came through the corruption of nature, therfore we flie from the same by the instinct of nature. These and the like fond reasons they alledge, for their excuse in flieng from their flocks, and charges, what say you to them?

Amphil. I can saie little to them. But onelie this, that none of all these reasons doe priuiledge them to discontinue from their flockes and charges. And whereas they saie, that their staieng were a tempting of God, it is verie vntrue, it is rather a reuerent obediéce to this tripled cómandement, Pasce oues meas, pasce oues meas, pasce oues meas, Feede my sheepe, feede my sheepe, feede my sheepe. But indeede if it were so that a priuate man who hath no

kind

kind of function no2 office, neither ecclesiasticall no2 tempo2all, seeing himselfe if he staie
stil in great danger of death, & might auoid the
danger by flieng, & so by the grace of God p2o-
long his life, and yet will not, this man if he
tarie tempteth the Lo2d, and is a martherer of
himselfe befo2e God. And to such it is said, thou
shalt keepe the whole from the sicke, & the sick
from the whole. This is the meaning & sence
of these wo2ds, and not that they do p2iuiledge
any man fo2 not doing of his dutie. But notwithstanding all that can be said in confutation of this great & extreeme contempt of their
duties, I haue knowne and doe know some
ministers (nay wolues in sheepes clothing) in
Dnalgne that in time of any plague, pestilence
o2 infection, thogh there hath bin no gret danger at all that haue bin so far from continuing
amongst their flock, ÿ if any one of them were
sicke, although of neuer so common o2 vsuall disease, yet fearing to be infected with the conta-
gion thereof they haue absented themselues altogither, from visiting ÿ sick acco2ding as they
ought, & as dutie doth bind them. Yea some of
them (suppose you of mercenaries, & hirelings,
but not of go d pasto2s) are so nice, so fine & so
fearefull of death fo2soth ÿ in no case they cannot abide to visit the sicke, neither by day no2

by night. But in my iudgement it is as incident to their office and dutie, to visite, to comfort, to instruct, and relieue the sicke, at the
houre of death, as it is for them to preach the
word of God to their flocke al the daies of their
life. And peraduenture they may doe more good
in one howre at the last gaspe, then they haue
done all the daies of their life before. For
he that in his life time hath had in small estimation the blessed worde of God, but following his owne humors in hope to liue long,
hath lead a very wicked and impenitent life,
nowe through the consideration and sight of
death, which he seeth before his eies, togither
with godly exhortations, admonitions, and
consolations, out of the word of God, may easelie be withdrawne from his former wicked
life, and dieng in the faith of Iesus Christ, with
true repentance for his sinnes, tofore committed, liue for euer in ioye both of body & soule,
whereas if exhortations had not bin, he might
(happily) haue died irrepentant, or vtterly des-
perate to his euerlasting destruction for euer.
Yea, it is commonly seene, that those who could
neuer be wonne to Christ Iesus, all the daies
of their life before, yet at the last howre they
are soone recouered. Therefore ought not the
pastors to neglecte their duties therein, but
warely

warely, and carefully to watche ouer their flocks, night and day without ceasing that whē the great shephard of the sheepe commeth, he may rewarde them with the immercessible crowne of eternall glory. And thus much be it spoken hereof.

Theod. In whome doth the election of the minister or pastor consist in the church onely or in the bishops?

Amphil. I tolde you before (as I remember) that the church might examine the life, the conuersation, and disposition of him, or them, whome they would haue to be their pastor, and finding the same good to present him, or them, to the bishops, or elders to whome it apperteineth, to examine for his sufficiencie in knowledge, and dexteritie, in teaching and handling the word of God, and finding him a man furnished with gifts and graces necessary for such a high vocation, to call him lawfullie according to the word of God, and so to sende him foorth into the Lords haruest, as a faithfull laborer therein.

Theod. But some are of opinion that the churches themselues of their owne absolute, and plenarie power ought to choose their pastor, and not bishops,

Ampil. The churches haue no further
power

power in the election of their pastor, than as I
haue told you, that is, to iudge of his conuersation & integritie of life, referring the whole
action besides to the bishops, and elders. For
if the churches should elect their minister or
pastor of themselues absolutely, besides that it
would breed confusion (for some would chuse
one, some another, some this, and some that, neuer contenting themselues with any) the church
should doe that also, which were directly contrarie to the word of God. For certeine it is
the church hath no absolute power by the word
of God to elect their pastor, to chuse him, to cal
him orderly in such forme as is appointed in
the word, obseruing all kinde of rites, ceremonies, & orders belonging thereto. Neither was
it euer seene that any church did euer practise
the same. For in the dais of the apostles did the
churches any more than chuse foorth certeine
persons of a tried conuersation, & presented thē
to the apostles? And did not the apostles then
whom our bishops now in this action do repre-
sent)lay their hands vpon them, approue them
(after triall had of their sufficiencie in knowledge)and sent them foorth into the Lords vineyard? The churches laid not their hands vpon
them, or as some call it consecrated them not,
nor vsed not any other ceremoniall rite in the
election

election of them, as the apostles did. But as I grant that the church for som cause, and in som respects is not to be excluded frō a consultatiue voyce (as before) or from being made priuie at al to the election of their pastor, so I denie that the church may absolutely of his owne plenarie power cal their pastor, all ceremonies and rites thereto belonging obserued, for that is to be don and executed of the bishops & elders, and not of the churches consisting of lay men, and for the most part rude, and vnlearned.

Theod. What say you to a seigniorie or eldership, were it not good for the state of the church at this day that ȳ same were established in euery congregation, as it was in ȳ apostles daies.

Amphil. The seueral estates and conditions of the apostolicall churches, and of ours (al circumstances duly considered) are diuers, and much different one from another, and therefore though a seigniorie or eldership then in euerie particular church were necessarie, yet now vnder christian princes it is not so nedfull. The churches then wanted christian princes and magistrates to gouerne the same, and therefore had need of some others to rule in the church. But God be thanked we haue most christian kings, princes, and gouernors, to rule and gouerne the church, & therfore we we stand in lesse néed of the other. And yet notwithstanding I grant that a seigniozie in euery congregation were to be wished, if it could be bzought to passe, yet cannot I perceiue, but that it would rather bzing confusion, than reformation, considering the state of the church at this day. Foz in the apostles times when seigniozies were ozdeined, we read not of any shires, dioces, oz pzecincts, where bishops and ecclesiasticall magistrates might exercise their authozitie and gouernement, as now they doe, and therefoze, there being neither bishops, ecclesiasticall noz ciuill magistrates (as we haue now) it was necessarie that the seigniozies shuld be ozdeined. But now we hauing al these things, stand not in such necessitie of them, as the churches in the apostles daies did. Besides, the institution of elders was but meere ceremoniall, and tempozall, and therefoze not to continue alwaies, neither ought the necessitie thereof to binde all churches. Neither doe I thinke that all churches are bound foz euer to one fozme of externall gouernement, but that euery church may alter, and change the same, accozding to the time, and pzesent state therof, as they shal see the same to make foz the glozie of God, and the common peace of the church.

Theod.

Theod. What say you to deacons ? Is their office necessarie or not in the church of God at this day?

Amphil. Their office (which was to make collections for the poore, to gather the beneuolencies, and contributions of euerie one that were disposed to giue, and to see the same bestowed vpon the poore and needie members of the church) is very necessarie, and without doubt ought to be continued for euer. But yet is not the church tied to their names onely, but to their office. Which office is executed by honest substantiall men (called Churchwardens or the like) chosen by the consent of the whole congregation to the same end and purpose, who daily gathering the friendlye beneuolencies of the churches, bestow, or see the same bestowed vpon the poore, and indigent of the same church, which was the greatest part of the deacons duties in the apostles daies. So that albeit wee haue not the name, we yet hold their office in substance and effect.

Theod. What is your iudgement, ought there to be any bishops in the churches of christians?

Amphil. To doubt whether there ought to be bishops in the churches of christians, is to doubt of the truth it selfe. For is there not

D. I.　　　　mention

mention made of their names, dignities, functions, and callings, almost in euery chapter of the new testament, in all the epistles of Paule, of Peter, of Iohn, of Iude, and of all the rest? Besides that did not the apostles themselues constitute and ordeine bishops and elders, and doe they not woonderfully commende the excellencie of their calling, inferring that those that rule well, are worthye of double honour? Whereby appeereth that bishops are not onlye needefull in the churches of christians, but also most needfull, as without whome I can scarcely see how the state of the church could well bee maintained. And therefore those that contend that they are not necessarie in a Christian Common wealth, shewe them selues either wilfull, waiwarde, or maliciouslye blinde, and striuing to catch their owne shadowes, they labour all in vaine, giuing manifest demonstration of their more than extreame follie to all the world.

Theod. Well. Let it bee granted (as it cannot bee denied) that they are moste necessarie, yet in this I would verie gladlye bee absolued, whether they maye lawfullye vendicate or challenge to themselues superioritie, and primacie aboue their fellowe
brethren

brethren of the ministerie or no, for some holde that there ought to bee equalitie in the ministerie, and no superioritie at all, how say you?

Amphil. They doe not vendicate or challenge anie superioritie or primacie to themselues ouer their brethren in respect of their common callings, and functions (for therein the poorest pastor or shepheard that is, is coequall with them, they themselues will not denie) but in respect of dignitie, authoritie, and honour, which the prince and church doth bestowe vpon them. So that the superioritie that they haue ouer their brethren, resteth in dignitie, authoritie, and honour, which it hath pleased the prince to dignifie them withall aboue their felowe brethren, and not in calling, function, or office, for therein they are all coequall togither. But if any curious heads should demand why the prince should aduance any of the cleargie to such high dignitie, authoritie, and primacie aboue his brethren, I answer as it is in the Gospel: Is thine eie euill, bicause the prince is good? May not the prince giue his gifts, his dignities, and promotions to whom he will? And if the prince of his roiall clemencie be minded to bestowe vpon his subiect any dignity or promotion, is it christian obedience

to refuse the same? Nay is it not extræme in-
gratitude towards his prince? Besides, who
seeth not, that if there should be no superioritie (I meane in dignitie, & authoritie only) the
same honorable office or calling would growe
into contempt? For is it not an old saieng, and
a true, Familiaritas, siue æqualitas parit con-
temptum, Familiaritie, or coequallitie doth e-
uer bring contempt. And therefore take awaye
authoritie, and honor from the magistrates either temporall or spirituall, and ouerthrowe
the same altogither. If authoritie should not be
dignified, as well with glorie, and externall
pompe the better to grace the same, & to shew
forth the maiestie thereof, would it not soone
grow to be dispised, bilipended and naught set
by? And therefore the more to innoble, and
set foorth the excellencie of this honorable calling of a bishop, hath the prince, & the churches
thought it good to bestow such authoritie, dignitie, and honor vpon them, and not for anie o-
ther cause whatsoeuer. And therefore seeing it
is the pleasure of the prince to bestowe such
dignitie, authoritie, and honor vpon them, me
thinke, any sober christians should easely tole-
rate the same.

    Theod. Yea, but they saie, that there
ought to be no superioritie in the ministerie,
                        bringing

himselfe. But whereas hée sayth that hee receiued his power of superioritie ouer all the worlde from no earthie creature, but from God himselfe, it is manifest that he receyued it neyther from God, (for his vsurped power is contrarie to God, and to his worde in euerie respecte) nor from anie christian man, but from the Deuill himselfe, whose vicegerent or Liefetenant generall in his kingedome of impietie he shewes himselfe to be. Than let them note, that although hée pretended to holde his vsurped authoritie from man (as hee doth not,) yet is there no man howe mightie an Emperour, King, Prince, or Potentate soeuer, that is able proprio iure to giue him authoritie ouer all the worlde, without great and manifeste iniurye done to all other Princes, as to giue the soueraigntie, or chieftie of their Landes from them, to a straunger. But a Prince may lawfullye bestowe, and geue to his subiectes anie prerogatiue, title, authoritie, office function, gouernment, or superioritie of anie thing within his owne dominions and kingdomes, but no further he maye not. And therefore this reason of theirs holdeth not, that the Pope maye as well arrogate the one to himselfe, as the Byshops may the other to themselues.

Theo.

Theod. Seeing now it cannot be denied, but that bishops are most necessarie, and that they may also lawfully hold superioritie ouer their brethren (in respect of gouernement, regiment or authoritie) being giuen them of the prince, what say you then to this? Whether may a bishop be called by the name of an archbishop, metropolitane, primate, or by the name of my Lord bishop, my Lords grace, the right honourable, and the like, or not? For me thinke these titles and names are rather peculiar to the temporaltie than to them, & do sauour of vainglorie, and worldly pompe, rather than of any thing else. And which is more, me thinke they are against the expresse word of God. Wherefore I couet greatly to heare your iudgement thereof?

Amphil. These names and titles may seeme to sauour of vaineglorie indeed, if they should arrogate them to themselues Iure diuino, as they doe not. But if you wil consider by whom they were giuen them, and how they doe require them, you wil not thinke it much amisse, nor farre discrepant from the sinceritie of the Gospell. First therefore note that they were giuen them by christian princes to dignifie, to innoble, to decore, and to set foorth the dignitie, the excellencie, and worthines of their callings.

the papiſts. For ſaie they the papiſts may as well affirme that chriſtian emperours kings, and potentates, and even the churches of God themſelues haue giuen to the pope that authoritie, that dignitie, and honor which he hath or claimeth aboue his fellowe brethren, as well as the biſhop may ſay ſo. Beſides it confirmeth the opinion of ſoueraigntie ouer al the churches in the world, For ſay they may not the pope ſaie that he receiued plenarie power to be head ouer all the world, from chriſtian kings, emperours, and potentates, as well as the biſhops may ſay, we receiued this power to be ſuperior to our brethren from chriſtian kings and princes. Now whether theſe reaſons be a like I would gladly know.

Amphil. They be verie vnlike, and ſo vnlike as there is no equallitie compariſon, or ſemblance betwixt them. For firſt of all let this note, that the pope nor any of his complices, and adherents doe not holde, nor pretende to holde (no they dare as well eate off their fingers as to ſay ſo, for then were their ſtate in a wofull caſe) that their archdiuell, their god the pope I ſhould ſay doth receiue his power either of authoritie, ſuperioritie, primacie, ſoueraigntie, or head ouer all the world from any earthly creature, but immediately from God himſelfe.

bringing in the example of the apostles themselues amongst whom was no superiozity, inequalitie, oz pzincipallitie at all?

-Amphil. Indeede amongst the apostles there was no superiozitie, I grant, neither in office calling, authozitie, noz otherwise, but al were equall in ech respecte, one to another. But what than? The apostles were sent to pzeach, to the churches, and not to gouerne (and therefoze rhey choose elders to rule the same.) but our bishops are as well to gouerne, and to rule the churches in some respects, as to pzeach the wozde. And therfoze though there were no superiozitie amongst the apostles, yet maye there be amongst our bishops in respect of gouerment, dignitie, and authozitie. And wheras they saie there ought to be no superiozitie in the ministerie at all, I answeare no moze there is in respect of euerie ones function, foze of calling, and office to pzeach the wozd and minister the sacraments. But in respect of gouernement, authozitie, dignitie, and honoz, there is superiozitie, and I am perswaded so ought to be. In which opinion, vntill they haue dispzooued it, I meane Chzist willing to persiste.

Theod. But they adde further, and say that it strengtheneth the hands of the aduersaries,

D.3.　　the

Amphil.   There is neither of the callings temporall, nor ecclesiasticall, but it requireth a whole and perfect man, to execute the same. And if there were neuer founde any one man yet so perfect, as could throughly, and absolutlie performe his office in either of the callings temporall or ecclesiastical, much lesse can there euer one man be found, that is able to discharg them both. It is hard therefore that these two callings should concurre in one man. This is as though a man hauing an importable burthen alreadie vpon his backe, should yet haue an other almost as burthenous vrged vppon him. And therefore as it were absurde to see a temporall magistrate mount into the pulpit, preach the worde, and minister the sacraments so absurde it is to see an ecclesiasticall magistrate exercise the authoritie temporall, and to giue sentence condemnatorie of life , & death, vpon any criminous person , which properlie belongeth to the temporall power. Besids, it is a great discredite to the temporall magistrate, because it may be thought that they are not wise nor politique inough to execute their office , nor discharge their duties without the aide, and assistance of the other .   And which is more it hindereth them from the discharge of their duties in their owne calling , for

it

ſtian, I holde them to be Chriſtian names, and geuen by Chriſtian Princes to the innobling and garniſhing of their offices, functions, and callinges, which doubtleſſe is a glorie to God denie it who will, or who can. And therefore in concluſion I ſay, that Byſhops though not by the lawe of God, yet by the poſitiue law, dona-tion, and gifture of Chriſtian Princes, maye lawfully aſſume the ſaide titles, and names to them for the cauſes before cited. And there-fore theſe names and titles bæing meere indif-ferent, and not derogating from the glorie of God, but rather making for the ſame, they are not of anye wiſe, ſober, or faythfull Chriſtian, neyther to bee inueighed againſt nor yet to bee in anye reſpecte diſlyked bæing vſed as before. And thus much of the names and titles of Byſhops.

Theodo.　Maye Byſhops exerciſe tempo-rall authoritie together with Eccleſiaſticall, and maye they bee Iuſtices of peace, Iuſtices of Quorum, Iuſtices of Aſſiſes, Ewer, De-terminer, and the lyke, or maye they as Capytall Iudges geue deſtructiue ſentence of lyfe and death vpon maleſactors and others, that by the iudiciall lawe of man haue deſerued to dye?

Amphil.

these and manie other the like places of holie
writt, it is cleare that they cannot arrogate
these names, or titles to themselues by $\tilde{y}$ word
of God, neyther doe they, but (as I haue said)
by the donation, the beneuolence, and gifture
of christian Princes for the reuerent estimati-
they bare and ought to beare to their high function and calling, in that they are his Liefete-
nants, his vicegerents in his Church, his mes-
sengers, his Ambassadors, the disclosers and
proclaimers of his secretes, and his Aungels,
(for so are they called in the scriptures) & therfore in respecte of the excellencie hereof, these
names were giuen and attributed vnto them.
And truely to speake my simple iudgement, I
sée not but that these names doe dignifie their
callinges, shewe forth the maiestie thereof, and
des moue the Churches to haue the same high
calling in more reuerence, & honor, than otherwise they would, if they were called by bare &
naked names onelie. But notwithstanding
either this that hath béene saide, or anie thinge
els that can be said herein, there are some wai-
ward spirits lately reuiued who hold the same
names to be méere Antichristian, blasphemous
and wicked, and suche as at anie hande a Minister of the Gospell ought not to bée called by.
But whereas they holde them to bée Antichristian,

lings . Secondly let them note that they require them as due vnto them by the donation and gifture of men, and not Iure diuino, and therefore being giuen them for the causes aforesaid by christian kings and princes, they may in that respect hold them still without any offence to the diuine goodnesse, or his faithfull spouse vpon the earth. But if they shuld claime them as due vnto them by the lawe of God, as they doe not, then should they offend. For our sauiour Christ seeing his disciples and apostles ambiciously to affect the same vainglorious titles and names, set before them the example of the heathen kings, thereby the rather to withdrawe them from their vaine humour, saieng : Reges gentium dominantur eis,&c. The kings of the gentils beare rule ouer them and those that exercise authoritie ouer them, be called gratious Lords, but Vos autem non sic, You shall not be so. In the which words he vtterly denieth them (and in them all others to the worlds end, that in the same office and function of life should succeed them) the titles of Lords, graces, or the like. The apostle also biddeth them to beware that they challenge not those vaine titles to themselues by the lawe of God, when he saith (speaking to bishops and pastors) Be not Lords ouer your flocks, &c. By

these

it is written, no man can serue two masters,
but either he must betraie the one or the other.
When the woman taken in adultery was apprehended, and brought vnto Christ, he refused
to giue iudgement of hir, and yet it was a matter in effect ecclesiasticall, & appertained to an
ecclesiasticall iudge. Then what ought they to
do in matters meere ciuil? Againe our sauior
Christ, when the yong man requested him to
deuide the inheritance betwixt his brother, &
him, refused the same saieng, Quis me consti-
tuit iudicem inter vos? Who made me a iudge
or a deuider betwixt you. Whereby appeareth
how farre ecclesiasticall persons ought to bee
frō hauing to doe, with temporal matters. But
whereas they say the bishops of Dnalgne do
exercise temporall authoritie, and doe it as
iudges capitall, giuing sentence condemnatorie of life, and death, it is verie vntrue otherwise than thus, to be present at the same, & to
haue a consultatiue exhortatiue, or consenta-
tiue voice onely. Which vse me thinkes is verie good and laudable in my iudgement. For
whereas the temporal magistrates not vnderstanding in euerie point the deapth of Gods
lawe if they shoulde doe anie thing either a-
gainst the same, or the lawe of a good conscience, they might informe tȝem thereof, that
all

all things might bee done to the glorie of God, the comforte of the poore members of Christe Jesus, and the benefit of the common welth.

Theodo. What fashion of apparell doe the pastors, and Ministers weare vsually in their common affaires?

Amphil. The same fashion that others doe for the most parte, but yet decente, and comlie, obseruing in euerie point a decorum. But as others weare their attire, some of this colour, some of that, some of this thinge, some of that, so they commonly weare all their apparell, at least the exteriour part of blacke colour, which as you know is a good, graue, sad, and auncient colour. And yet notwithstanding herein some of them (I speake not of all) are muche to bee blamed, in that they cãnot content themselues with cõmon, and vsuall fashions, but they must chop and chaunge euerie day with the worlde. Yea some of them are as fonde in excogitating deuising and inuenting of new fashions euerie day, & in wearing the same, as the veriest Royster of them all. And as they are faultie in this respect, so are they herein to be blamed, in that they cannot contente themselues with cloth though neuer so excellent, but they must weare silkes, veluets, satans, damaskes, grograms, taffeties, and the like. I speake not agaynst those

those that are in authoritie for wearing of these thinges (for they both maie, and in some respectes ought to weare them for the dignifiyng of their offices and callings, which otherwise mighte growe into contempte) but against those that bée meane pastours, and Ministers, that flaunt it out in their saten doblets, taffette doblets, silke hosen, garded gownes, cloakes, and the like. Alas howe shoulde they rebuke pryde, and excesse in others, who are as faultye therein as the reste? Therefore sayde Cato verye well, Quæ culpare soles, ea tu ne feceris ipse : for sayeth he, Turpe est doctori, cum culpa redarguit ipsum. Which is, those thinges which thou blamest in others, sée that thou thy selfe bee not guiltye in the same, for it is a foule blemish and a great shame and discredit, when that euill which thou reprouest in an other, is apparent in thy selfe. For in so doing, a man reprehendeth as well himselfe as others, is a hinderance to the course of the Gospell, and what he buildeth with one hand, he pulleth down with the other. Christ Iesus the great pastor of the shéepe was himself contéted to go daily in one poore coat, béeing knit, or wouen all ouer without séeme, as the maner of ỹ Palistinians is to this day. This me think was but a simple cote

in

in the eie of the world, and yet Christ Iesus thought it pretious inough. Samuel was accustomed to walke in an olde gowne girded to him with a thong. Elias and Elizeus in a mantell, Iohn the baptist in camels haire with a girdle of a skin about his loines. The apostle Paule with a poore cloke, and the like, wherby appeareth, how farre a minister of the Gospell ought to be from pride, and worldly vanitie, obseruing the rules of christian sobrietie, as well in apparell, as in al things else, knowing that he is as a citie set vppon an hill, and as a candle set vppon a candlesticke to giue light, and shine to al the whole church of God. Therfore saith Christ : Sic luceat lux vestra coram hominibus, &c. Let your light so shine before men, that they seeing your good workes, may glorifie your father which is in heauen : which God grant we may all doe.

Theod. Haue they no other kind of apparell different from the common sort of men?

Amphil. Yes marie haue they. They haue other attire more proper, and peculiar vnto them (in respect of their functions and offices) as cap, tippet, surplesse, and the like. These they weare, not commonly, or altogither, but in especial when they are occupied in, or about the execution of their offices and callings, to

this

this end end purpose, that there may be a difference betwixte them, and the common sorte of
people, and that the one maie be distincte from
the other by this outward note or marke.

Theodo. Is it of necessitie than required,
that the Pastors and Ministers of the worde,
should be distincted from other people, by anie
severall kind of attire?

Amphil. It is not required as of necessitie,
bnt thought mæte and convenient to bee vsed
for a decencie, and comlines in the Church of
God. But notwithstanding the chiefest thyng
wherby a pastor or minister oght to be known
from the common, & vulgare sorte of people is,
the preaching of the word of God, the administration of the sacraments, the execution of ecclesiasticall discipline, and other censures of the
Church, and withall his integritie of lyfe, and
soundnesse of conuersation in euerie respecte.
These are the true notes, and markes wherby
a Minister of the Gospell ought to bee knowen
and distincted from the other common sorte of
people. And yet though these bee the chiefest
notes whereby they are distinct from others of
the temporaltie and laitie, yet are they not the
onelie notes, or markes, for they are knowen
and discerned from others also, by exteriour habite, and attire, as namely by cappe, tippet, sur

P. I.   plesse

plesse, and such like : That as the first doth distinguish them from others, whilest they are er-
ercised about the same, (for who is so doltishe
that seeing a man preache, minister the sacraments, & execute other ecclesiasticall censures
of the church, that will not iudge him to bee a
Minister of the Gospell?) so the other notes of
apparell (the surplesse except) may make a difference, and distinguishe them from others of
the laitie abroad. To this end, that the reuerēce
which is due to a good pastor, or minister of the
Gospell may be giuen vnto them. For as the
Apostle saith, those elders that rule well, are
worthie of double honour.

Theod. But I haue heard great disputation
and reasoning pro & contra, to and fro, that
the pastors and ministers of the Gospell, ought
not to be disseuered from the common sorte of
people, by anie distincte kinde of apparell, but
rather by sounding the Lordes voice on high,
by ministring the sacramentes, and the like,
what say you to the same?

Amphil. Indæde there are some I confesse,
that are of that opinion, and they bring in the
example of Saule, enquiring of Samuell
for the seers house, inferring that the Prophet was not distinct from other common people in his attire, for than Saule should easelie
haue

haue knowen him by the ſame. And the example of the damoſell, that ſpake to Peter, inferring that whereas the mayde ſayde, Thy ſpeech bewrayeth thee, if he had bene diſtincte from others in attire, or outwarde apparell, ſhee would than haue ſayd, Thy apparel ſheweth thee to bee ſuch a fellowe. Theſe with the like examples they pretende to prooue that paſtors and Miniſters are not to bee diſcerned and knowen from the lay people, by anye kinde of apparell. But as I will not ſaie that they are to bee knowen, and diſcerned from others by apparell or habite onelye, (but rather by the lifting vp of their voices like Trumpetes as ſaith the Prophet) ſo I wyll not denye the ſame to bee no note or marke at all to knowe a Paſtour or Miniſter of the Goſpell by from others of the temporaltie, and laitie. And truelye for my parte, I ſee no great inconuenience, if they bee by a certaine kinde of decente habite (commaunded by a Chriſtian Prince) known and diſcerned from others. Yet ſome more curious than wiſe, before they would weare anie diſtinct kind of apparell from others, they haue rather choſen to render vp both liuinges, goods, families, and all, leauing their flockes to the mouth of the wolues.

P.2.   Theo.

Theod. Is it lawfull for a minister of th Gospell to weare a surplesse, a tippet or forked cappe, and the like kind of attire?

Amphil. As they are commaunded by the Pope the great Antichrist of the worlde, they ought not to weare them, but as they be commaunded, and inioyned by a Christian Prince, they maie weare them without scruple of conscience. But if they should repose any religion, holinesse or sanctimonie in them, as the doting Papists doe, than doe they grœuouslie offende, but wearing them as things mœre indifferent (although it be controuersiall whether they bœ things indifferente or not) I sœ no cause why they maie not vse them.

Theod. From whence came these garments can you tell, from Rome, or from whence els?

Amphil. The most hold that they came first from Rome, the poison of all the world, & most likelie they did so, but other some searching the same more narrowlie, do hold y they came not from Rome, but rather from Grecia, which frō the beginning for the most part, hath euer bœn contrarie to the Church of Rome. But from whence soeuer they came it skilleth not much, for bœing mere indifferent, they maie be worn or not worne without offence, according to the pleasure of the Prince, as things which of thē-

selues

ſelues bee not euill, noꝛ cannot hurte, excepte
they be abuſed.

Theod. Notwithſtanding they holde this foꝛ
a maxime, that in as much as they came firſt
from the Papiſtes, and haue of them bæne ido-
latrouſlie abuſed, that therefoꝛe they are not,
noꝛ ought not to bee vſed of anie true paſtoꝛs,
oꝛ Miniſters of the Goſpell. Is this their aſſumption true, oꝛ not?

Amph. It is no good reaſo̅ to ſay ſuch a thing
came from the Papiſtes, ergo it is naught. Foꝛ
we read that the Deuils confeſſed Jeſus Chꝛiſt
to be the ſonne of God, doth it follow therefoꝛe
that the ſame pꝛofeſſion is naughts, becauſe a
wicked creature vttered the ſame? All thinges
are therefoꝛe to bee examined, whether the a-
buſe conſiſt in the thinges themſelues, oꝛ in o-
thers that abuſe them. Which being found out,
let the abuſes be remoued, and the thinges remaine ſtill. A wicked man maye ſpeake good
woꝛdes, doe good woꝛks befoꝛe the woꝛld, (but
becauſe they wante the oile of faith to ſouple
them withall, they are not good woꝛkes befoꝛe
the Loꝛd) and maie oꝛdaine a good thing which
maie ſerue to good ends, and purpoſes. And becauſe the ſame hath afterward bæne abuſed,
ſhall the thing it ſelfe therefoꝛe be quite taken
away? No, take away the abuſe, let the thinge

remaine

remaine ſtill, as it maye very well without anie offence, except to them, quibus omnia dantur ſcandalo , to whom all thinges are offence.
And further, if theſe preſicians would haue all
things removed out of the Church which haue
béene abuſed to Idolatrie , than muſt they pull
downe Churches, (for what hath bene abuſed
more to Idolatrie and ſuperſtition?) pulpits,
belles, and what not . Than muſt they take away the vſe of bread and wine, not onely from
the church, but alſo from the vſe of man in this
life, becauſe ẏ ſame was abuſed to moſt ſhame
full idolatrie , in béeing dedicate to Ceres, and
Bacchus, twoo ſtinking Idols of the Gentiles.
Than muſt they take away not onely the Epi
ſtles, and Goſpels , but alſo the whole volume
of the holy ſcriptures , becauſe the Papiſtes abuſed them to idolatrie. By all which reaſons
with infinite the like, it manifeſtly appeareth,
that manie things which haue beene inſtituted
by Idolaters , or by them abuſed to Idolatrie,
may be applied to good vſes , and may ſerue to
good ends, ẏ abuſes being takē away. Yet wold
I not that any thing that hath béen idolatrouſly
abuſed by the papiſts, ſhould be reteined in the
churches of Chriſtians , if by any meanes they
might be removed, and better put in place.

Theodo. Is the wearing of theſe garments

a

a thing mœre indifferent, oꝛ not? foꝛ some hold
it is, some hold it is not?

Amph. It is a thing ẁout al cõtrouersẏ mere
indifferent, foꝛ whatsoeuer gods woꝛd neither
expꝛessly cõmandeth, neither direaly foꝛbiddeth,
noꝛ whiꝛh bindeth not ẏ conscience of a chꝛiſtian man, is a thing mere indifferent to be vsed,
oꝛ not to be vsed, as the pꝛeſẽt ſtate of ẏ church,
ẛ time requireth. But it is certen that the wea
ring of this kind of attire is not expꝛessly commanded in the woꝛd of God, noꝛ direaly foꝛbid
by the same, ẛ therfoꝛe is mere indifferent, and
may be vsed, oꝛ not vsed ẁithout burthẽ of cõ-
science, as ẏ pꝛesent ſtate of time shall require.
And therfoꝛe ſœing they be things indifferent,
I wold wish euery wise chꝛiſtiã to tollerate ẏ
same, being certen that he is neither better noꝛ
woꝛſe, foꝛ wearing oꝛ not wearing of them.

Theod. Being things as you say mere indifferent, may any man lawfully refuse ẏ wearing
of thẽ againſt the cõmandement of his pꝛince,
whom next vnder God he ought to obey?

Amphil. Euery man is bound in conscience
befoꝛe God to obey his pꝛince in all things, yea
in things directly contrary to true godlines hœ
is boũd to shew this obediéce (but not to cõmit
ẏ euil) namely to submit himselfe life, lands, liuings, oꝛ els whatsoeuer he hath to ẏ wil of his
                    P.4.   Pꝛince,

Princes,rather then to disobeie. If this obedience than be due to Princes in matters,contrarie to true godlinesse , what obedience than is due to thē in matters of small waight,of small importaunce , and mēere trifles as these garments be,iudge you? He that disobeieth the cōmaundement of his Prince,disobeieth the commaundement of God, and therfore would God all Ecclesiasticall persons that stande so muche vpon these small pointes , that they breake the common vnitie,& band of charitie in the church of God,{would nowe at the last qualifie themselues,shewe obedience to Princes lawes,and fall to preaching of Christ Iesus truelie , that his kingdome might dailie bee increased,their consciences discharged , and the Church edefied , which Christe Iesus hath bought with the shedding of his precious hart bloud.

   Theod. Maie a pastor,or a Minister of the Gospell forsake his flocke,and refuse his charge for the wearing of a surplesse , a cappe , tippet, or the like , as manie haue done of late daies, who being inforced to weare these garmentes, haue giuen vp their liuings , and forsaken all?

   Amphil. Those that for the wearing of these garments,being but the inuentions,the traditions,the rites,the ceremonies,the ordinances & constitutions of man,will leaue their flocks,
and

and giue ouer their charges, not caring what become of the same, doe shew themselues to be no true shepheards, but such as Christ speaketh of, that when they see the Wolfe comming will flie away, leauing their flocke to the slaughter of the greedie wolfe. They giue euident demonstration also, that they are not such as the holie Ghost hath made ouerseers ouer their flocke, but rather such as being possessed with the spirite of pride and ambition, haue intruded themselues, to the destruction of their flocke. If they were such good shepheards as they ought to be, and so louing to their flocke, they would rather giue their life for their sheepe if neede required, than to runne from them, leauing them to the bloodie teeth of the mercilesse wolues. Is hee a good shepheard that watcheth dailie vppon his flocke, or hee that runnes from them for euerie light trifle? I thinke we would count him a verie negligent shepheard. And shall wee thinke him a diligent, or a good pastor, and one that would giue his life for his sheepe, as a good pastor should doe, that for such trifles wil estrang himselfe from his flocke for euer? Therefore I beseech God to giue them grace to looke to their charges, and to let the other trifles alone, being no part of our saluation or damnation.

    Theod. But they saie they refuse the wearing

ring of these garments, because they are offensiue to the godlie, a scandall to the weake brethren, a hinderaunce to manie in comming to the Gospel, & an induration to the papists hardning their hearts, in hope that their trumperie will once come in again to their singular comfort.

Amphil. It is an old saying. Better a bad excuse, than none at all. And truly it seemeth they are driuen to the wall, and sore graueled, that will flie to these simple shifts. But whatsoeuer they say or affirme, certain it is, that offensiue to the godly they cannot be, who haue already learned to distinguish betwixt the things abused, and the abuses themselues. And who know also how to vse things mere indifferent to good ends, and purposes. And therfore this question thus I shut vp in few words, that the wearing of these garmentes being commaunded by a Christian Prince, is not offensiue, or scandalous to anie good Christians, and to the other it mattereth not what it be. For they are such as the Lorde hath cast off into a reprobate sence, and preiudicate opinion, abusing all things, euen the truth it selfe to their owne destruction for euer excepte they repent, which I praye God they maye doe, if it bee his blessed will.

Theo.

Theodo. I pray you why doe they weare
white in their surplesses, rather than any other
colour? and why a forked cappe rather than a
rounde one, for the Papiſtes (if they were
the authors of theſe garmentes) haue their
miſteries, their figures, & their repreſentations
in all things. Wherfore I deſire to know your
iudgment herein.

Amphil. You ſay the truth, for the Papiſtes
haue their miſteries in all things after their
maner. Therfore thus they ſay that white doth
ſignify holines, innocency, & al kind of integri-
ty, putting them in mind what they ought to be
in this life, and repreſenteth vnto them the beatitude, the felicitie, and happines of the life to
come . And thys they prooue ab exemplis
apparitionum, from the example of apparitiōs
and viſions, in that aungels, and celeſtial creatures haue euer appeared in the ſame colour
of white. Therefore forſooth they muſt weare
white apparell . The cornered cappe ſay theſe
miſterious fellows doth ſignifie, and repreſent
the whole monarchy of the world, Eaſt, Weſt,
North, & South, the gouernment whereof ſtan-
deth vpon them, as the cappe doth vppon their
heades . The gowne ſaye they doth ſignifie
the plenary power which they haue to doe all
things. And therefore none but the Pope, or hée
with

with whome hee dispenceth, maie weare the same euerie where, bicause none haue plenari-am potestatem plenarie power in euerie place, but (Beelzebub) the Pope. Yet the Ministers saith he, maie weare them in their Churches, & in their owne iurisdictions', because therein they haue full power from him. Thus foolishlie do they deceiue themselues with vaine shewes, shadowes, and imaginations, forged in the mint of their owne braines to the destruction of ma-nie. But who is he, that because these sottishe Papistes haue and doe græuouslie abuse these thinges, will therefore haue them cleane re-moued? If all thinges that haue beene abused should be remooued because of the abuse, than should we haue nothing left to the supply of our necessities, neither meat, drinke, nor cloth for our bodies, neyther yet (which is more) the word of God, the spirituall food of our soules, nor any thing els almost. For what thing is there in the whole vniuersall world, that eyther by one He-reticke or other hath not bene abused? Let vs therfore take the abuses away, and the things maie well remaine still. For may not we chri-stians vse these thinges which the wicked Pa-pists haue abused to good ends, vses, and purpo-ses? I sœ no reason to the contrarie. And there-fore in conclusion I besœch the Lorde that wee

may

may all agrée togither in one truth, and not to deuide our selues, one from another for trifles, making schismes, ruptures, breaches, and factions in the church of God, where we ought to nourish peace, vnitie, concord, brotherly loue, amitie, and frendship, one amongst an other. And seeing we do all agree togither, and iump in one truth, hauing al one God our father, one Lord Iesus Christ our sauiour, one holy spirit of adoption, one price of redemption, one faith, one hope, one baptisme, and one and the same inheritance in the kingdome of heauen, Let vs therefore agree togither in these externall shadowes, ceremonies, and rites. For is it not a shame to agree about the marow, and to striue about the bone? to contend about the karnell, & to vary about the shell? to agree in the truth, and to brabble for the shadow? Let vs consider that this contention of ours among our selues, both hinder the course of the Gospell from taking such deepe roote in the heartes of the hearers, as otherwise it would doe. And thus for this time brother Theodorus, we will breake off our talke concerning this matter, vntill yt please God that we may meete againe. Which if it please God we doe, I promise you in an other woorke to discourse of the same more at large. In the mean time let vs giue our selues to fasting, and prayer, most humbly beseeching his excellent maiesty to blesse our noble Queen, and to keepe hir grace as the apple of his eie frõ all hir foes, to maintaine his word, and gospell amongst vs, to plant vnity, and concord within our walles, to increase our faith, to graunt vs true and vnfained repentaunce for our sins, and in the end eternall life in the kingdome of heauen, thorow ý precious death, passion, blood-shedding, and obedience of Christe Iesus our Lord, and onely sauiour, to whom with the father and the holy ghost, one true, and immortal God, be al honor, praise, power, empire, and dominion throughout all congregations for euer-more. And thus brother Theodorus I bid you farewell in the Lord, till I do see you againe.

Theodo. And I you also good brother Amphilogus, beseeching the Lord that if we meete not vpon earth, we maye meete yet in the kingdome of heauen, there to rest in perfect felicitie for euer.

Amphil. The Lord grant it for his mercies sake.

Amen.

FINIS.

LONDON

Printed by Roger

VVard for VVilliam Wright,

and are to be solde at his shop ioy-
ning to Saint Mildreds Church in
the Poultry, being the mid-
dle shop in the row.

1583.

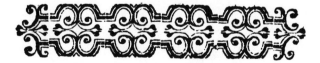

Appendix

Cancel title page from BM Grenville 10370.

THE
Second part
of the Anatomie of

Abuses, contaning The display
of Corruptions, with a perfect de-
scription of such imperfections, blemishes, and abuses, as now reigning in euerie degree, require reformation for feare
of Gods vengeance to be powred vpon
the people and countrie, without
speedie repentance. and con-
uersion vnto God : made
dialogwise by Phil-
lip Stubbes.

Except your righteousnes exceed the righteousnes of the Scribes and Phari-
ses, you cannot enter into the
kingdome of heauen.

LONDON.

Printed by R.W. for William Wright,
and are to be sold at his shop ioining
to S. Mildreds Church in the
Poultrie, being the mid-
dle shop in the rowe.